"Whether you're a laborer, foreman, or head of the firm, your lot in life is by no means guaranteed. 'Good enough' no longer is, and even if you're great, you're going to have to let other people know—not once in a while but all the time. This book will show you how to do just that: how to pitch to win—and get what you want out of your career, your job, your life."

—from **THE PERFECT PITCH**

THE EXPERTS AGREE: *THE PERFECT PITCH* WILL LAND YOU THE JOB OF YOUR DREAMS!

"You'll laugh out loud while you learn the hip, happening steps to pitch your idea and yourself."

—D.A. Benton,
author of *How to Think Like a CEO*

"The perfect tool for anyone who needs to market themselves. In addition to his invaluable, step-by-step information, David Andrusia's humor and down-to-earth style are delightful. I learned and laughed and can't wait to go pitch myself."

—Jill Spiegel,
author of *Flirting for Success*

more . . .

The
Perfect
Pitch

How to Sell Yourself
for Today's Job Market

David Andrusia

WARNER BOOKS

A Time Warner Company

Copyright © 1997 by David Andrusia
All rights reserved.

Warner Books, Inc., 1271 Avenue of the Americas, New York, NY 10020

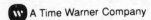 A Time Warner Company

Visit our Web site at http://warnerbooks.com

Printed in the United States of America
First Printing: November 1997
10 9 8 7 6 5 4 3 2 1

Library of Congress Cataloging-in-Publication Data

Andrusia, David.
   The perfect pitch : how to sell yourself for today's job market / David Andrusia.
     p. cm.
   ISBN 0–446–67294–7
   1. Vocational guidance.   2. Job hunting.   3. Assertiveness (Psychology)
   4. Persuasion (Psychology)   I. Title.
   HF5381.A7845   1997
   650.14—dc21   96–48246
                                               CIP

Book design and text composition by Ralph Fowler
Cover design by Irving Freeman

Contents

Prologue   vii

Acknowledgments   ix

1 Introduction   1

2 What Is a Pitch and Why Do I Need One?   7

3 What Can I Pitch?   15

4 Necessity Is the Mother of Invention or
How I Learned to Pitch   17

5 Seven Steps to a Perfect Pitch   24

6 Creating Your Personal Perfect Pitch:
A Step-by-Step Guide   32

7 Sleuthing: Uncovering Hidden Jobs
Even Before They Occur   71

8 Pitching in Response to Job Ads or
You *Will* Be Seen!   93

9 Pitching to Recruiters and Search Firms   105

10 Pitching to Employment Agencies   120

11 Temporary Solutions   126

12 Pitching for Promotions . . .
        Or Keeping the Job You Have   137

13 Pitching to Change Careers   148

14 The College Pitch   167

15 Networking:
        The Perfect Pitcher's Lifetime Tool   174

16 The Paper Pitch: Your Résumé   194

17 The In-Person Pitch: Interview to Win!   206

18 The Perfect Freelance/Consulting Pitch or
        Downsized but Not Out!   220

19 Persistence: The Truly Perfect Pitch   240

        Appendix:
        Employment Reference Sources   243

        About the Author   256

Prologue

Been there, done that, seen 'em all. As a one-time job seeker and all-the-time career consultant, I've read practically every guide to getting a job that's ever been writ. Some tell you what kind of shoes to wear, others how to shake hands, and some have the audacity to proffer personal points of view on whether or not a nose job will help you get a job.

Most of these books are big on spiritual shtick, tossing around aphorisms, adages, and assorted bon mots like confetti on New Year's Eve. One even takes a religious point of view, beseeching readers to put themselves in the hands of God as a means of ensuring career success.

I agree: Faith is important, and studies show that true believers live longer, healthier lives. But it's belief in *yourself* as well as a higher power, not a fatalistic fervor, that will help get the job, project, or consultancy of your dreams.

So get out of the kitchen; you'll find no chicken soup for the soul here. And I'm afraid you'll have to check *Bartlett's Familiar Quotations* for words of wonder and warmth. This is where you'll find the *real* feel-good stuff: the secrets, stripped to their essence, of the Andrusia Technique—your road to the Perfect Pitch and the work you've always wanted to have.

Acknowledgments

My heartfelt thanks to:

Rob McQuilkin, who acquired this book and was the first to share the Perfect Pitch vision

Diane Stockwell, gifted editor, great friend, and ardent supporter—here's to the first of many!

Karen Thompson, for doing a magnificent job on the copy editing (Scorpios rule!)

All my friends, family, and clients (you know who you are)

And, most of all, to my dear friend and agent, Katharine Sands—a pitchmistress par excellence who never let me give up the dream that this book was always meant to be.

The Perfect Pitch

1
. . .

Introduction

Several years ago, as head of marketing for a Hollywood film studio's home video group, I needed to hire a marketing manager. The company was supertrendy, the salary was great, the offices were smashingly designed, and the work was fulfilling and fun. In sum: It was the job of anyone's dreams.

To fill the position, I placed ads in the *Hollywood Reporter* and *Daily Variety,* the entertainment industry's main trade papers, told everyone I knew to send me great candidates, and conducted a survey of my own to source junior video marketing people who might want to make a move. So I got hundreds of résumés with fabulous cover letters from job seekers telling me why they were the hottest thing since cream cheese and why they wanted the job. Right?

Wrong. What I got was a pile of standard-issue résumés with cover notes as bland as bread: a virtual catalog of phrases from production-line résumé preparers, all lacking in imagination, enthusiasm, and personal flair. And precious few even bothered to tell me what they'd done for their previous employer and what superior creatures they themselves were.

Letters like this one:

> Mr. David Andrusia
> NEW LINE HOME VIDEO
> Los Angeles, CA
>
> Dear Mr. Andrusia:
>
> I am responding to your company's notice for a marketing manager that appeared in the *Hollywood Reporter.*
>
> I am currently employed as a marketing manager at ABC Advertising on the Honda campaign. In addition to a five-year marketing career, I procured my MBA at Degree Mill University.
>
> I believe I possess all the qualities required for success in the advertised position. Please call me if you would like to discuss this further.
>
> Thank you.
>
> Sincerely,
>
> Carla Clueless

Letter, how do I hate thee? Let me count the ways:

1. The overall tone is generic, without any attention paid to the advertisement—and position—at hand. (The ad listed a full set of basic qualifications; instead of showing how she had contributed in all these areas, Carla made reference to none.)

2. The writing style is banal and, in several instances, un-grammatical. If the syntactical errors don't cry out to you, chances are you need to brush up on your English skills. (Note: Prostitutes procure customers; one does not procure a degree.)

3. Nearly every sentence begins with "I." In addition to being stylistically boring, it represents a rather narcissistic point of view. Prospective employers don't care what *you* want; they want to know what you can do for *them*.

4. If your academic qualifications are splendid, mention them in the cover letter. If you attended a school of no particular note, don't.

5. "Please call me?" I don't think so! Never end with a plea; instead, it's incumbent on you to tell your potential boss exactly what you can do for him or her, e.g., "I would welcome the opportunity to meet you to discuss how I can help take New Line Home Video to new vistas in market position and—more important—sales." (Now *that's* a closing that will generate interviews!)

While Carla's letter was certainly among the most egregious I received, it was far from atypical. The lion's share of documents I received were cookie-cutter résumés that said absolutely nothing to me.

When I finally selected a set of people to see, I was more than ready to be wowed—to have candidates tell me why they could do a bang-up job and why they wanted to work at one of the hottest companies in town. Instead, what I got was a lot of smiling faces and passive points of view.

These were potentially excellent candidates, all with superior professional backgrounds, most with top-ten MBAs. Yet not one of these candidates had found their Perfect Pitch. Not one knocked me over with their overwhelming desire to work for New Line Home Video or was able to tell me clearly and succinctly what they could do for me.

As the weeks passed, and my frustration level grew, I expressed my amazement to my assistant and, increasingly, confidante, Michele B. (Though she had only been on board for two months, and had actually started as a temp, I recognized her drive and talent, and snapped her up as soon as funding for a permanent position was approved.)

"Maybe it's an L.A. thing," I mused. "Maybe I'm just looking for that quick-witted, fast-moving New York attitude—that certain spark that I'm just not going to find out here."

"But I'm from L.A.," Michele offered. "And if I may be so bold, you're ready to sing my praises at the drop of a hat."

"That's true. But you went to college back East; and besides, your mother's Jamaican. That West Indies repartee is as sharp as any New Yorker's razor tongue!"

"True." (Pregnant pause.) "So why don't you hire me?"

"Michele, you know I think the world of you. But I'm really looking for five years' marketing experience and a top-drawer MBA."

"I understand. Still, who managed most of the *Critters 3* campaign?"

"You did, and you did a wonderful job. But that was a little film, and I need substantial experience to handle our 'A' titles."

"So hire that person for 'A' films. And let me do the marketing on the lower-budget releases."

Unprepared for this proposal—this *pitch*—I was left momentarily speechless. If it's one thing the progressive executive knows, it's never to say no to a new idea without giving it due thought. (Of course, far too many managers do exactly this; it's the greatest pitfall of the conformist corporate world.)

"Let me think about it." I half-smiled.

"Fair enough. And in the meantime, would you seriously object to my writing a marketing plan for *Freddy's Dead*?"

I had planned to write that plan myself over the weekend. And who was I to object to a little bit of responsibility taken off my shoulders?

"Sure, be my guest. But, Michele—no promises."

"No promises," she agreed, and returned to her desk grinning from ear to ear.

• • •

The end of this story is hardly obscure; you surely guessed its outcome paragraphs ago. On Monday morning, I returned to the office to find a fully fleshed marketing plan on my chair, one in which I could find no fault. Yet still I was hesitant; Michele just didn't have the range of experience I was looking for.

When we met later in the day, I told her so—and admitted I was impressed by what she had written.

"I think you're terrific, Michele; I'm just looking for a more experienced marketing manager," I confided.

"Then make me assistant marketing manager," she offered. "Linda downstairs has that title, and she was promoted from assistant. I'll handle the B titles, which I'm doing anyway, and you can hire a hotshot MBA to market the big guns."

A brilliant idea; why hadn't I thought of it first? I, in turn, pitched this solution to my boss, who could find no good reason to say no, and Michele got the promotion she convinced me she deserved.

She had, in fact, made a *perfect pitch*. And no matter what your field, what your age, or where you live, you can too.

Sound too easy, too good to be true? Once you know the secrets of pitching, you'll wonder how you ever did business before. Yet, after fifteen years as an executive with major companies, I'm constantly amazed at how few people know how a pitch—for an assignment, a project, a job—can mean the difference between being an almost-ran and winning big. You only need to consider the parade of job applicants in the example above to see how powerful a Perfect Pitch can be.

So discard all your preconceived notions about how to get a job; toss out the tried and true. This is about a whole new way of getting and keeping the job of your dreams, even in these turbulent times. It's about finding your own Perfect Pitch.

2
...

What Is a Pitch and Why Do I Need One?

To be perfectly honest, you didn't always need to pitch. Oh, sure, people in sales, carnival barkers, and such have always pitched for a living, but for a steady gig in the corporate world, pitching used to be icing on the cake, not a necessary part of business life. America was expanding, companies needed staff, and unless you were a sociopath, an ax murderer, or had a religious aversion to brushing your teeth, there was always a place for you.

Unfortunately, unless you've been living under a rock (or have a trust fund that makes work just another four-letter word), you've already found out that a steady gig—much less the charmingly antiquated notion of lifetime employment—is by no means a sure thing anymore. The white-collar life of Daddy bringing home the bacon with an easy nine-to-five job—and bringing home much more than that with a college degree—is a notion that's just about bitten the dust for good. Or, to borrow an oft-circulated joke:

The status symbol of the eighties was a BMW.

The status symbol of the nineties is a job.

Indeed, in his critically acclaimed book *The End of Afflu-ence: The Causes and Consequences of America's Economic Dilemma,* Jeffrey Madrick notes that, in the nineties,

> *an increasing proportion of workers couldn't find jobs. The aver-age unemployment rate climbed from 4.5 percent in the 1950s . . . to 7.3 percent in the 1980s, and has averaged between 6 and 7 percent so far in the 1990s. As many as one million Americans left the workforce entirely, and were no longer counted among the un-employed.*

Blue-collar layoffs were nothing new; since the advent of the Industrial Revolution, jobs swelled and shrank with supply and demand. Much more telling is the effect that retrenchment has had on the previously unscathed ranks of the professional world. As Madrick notes, "By about 1987 slow economic growth had begun to put pressure on the salaries of better-paid white-collar workers as well." And, moreover, that "slow growth since 1973 [has] resulted in the loss of several million jobs."

Discouraging figures, these; but, of course, if you've been out in the job market recently, you already know the score. The reasons are much discussed and myriad, but the principal ones are obvious: Companies have reduced the sizes of their work-forces more dramatically than ever before; the dollar buys less, requiring more than one person in a family to work; and our larger population lives longer and requires a greater number of jobs. Plus, there's this indisputable fact:

The proportion of white males who had graduated from college rose from 6 percent in 1947 to 11 percent in 1955 and to about 25 percent in the 1980s. (Bureau of Census figures)

This figure of college graduates (a higher figure than any other industrialized country, in part due to lower standards for university admission vis-à-vis, say, those in France or Germany) and a loss of manufacturing jobs by themselves point to a lower ratio of people to jobs. Add to that a trend not acknowledged by the census figure above—the positive social change of African and Hispanic Americans (not so long ago relegated to agricultural and unskilled posts) entering the professional workforce—and what you've got is more Americans than ever vying for an increasingly shrinking number of jobs.

And that's just the beginning. According to Jeremy Rifkin's cautionary book *The End of Work:*

Global unemployment has now reached its highest level since the great depression of the 1930s. More than 800 million human beings are now unemployed or underemployed in the world.

Moreover:

Already, millions of workers have been permanently eliminated from the economic process, and whole job categories have shrunk, been restructured, or disappeared.

This point of view is shared by Madrick, who notes, "The re-engineering of work is eliminating jobs of all kinds and in greater number than at any time in recent memory." And, closer to home, the news isn't getting any better: "In the United

States, corporations are eliminating more than two million jobs annually."

This is a view shared by no less esteemed a source than the *New York Times,* whose widely hailed seven-part series on the downsizing of America proclaimed:

> *More than 96 million jobs have been erased in the United States since 1979. . . . increasingly the jobs that are disappearing are those of higher-paid, white-collar workers, many at large corporations.*

It's a sentiment Madrick echoes: "More people of all ages, no matter what their ethnic group or educational qualifications, have lost jobs than at any other time in the postwar era."

But what about the bazillions of new jobs the President touts on the evening news? Well, according to Charles Derber in *The Wilding of America,* "Forty-four percent of the new jobs created in the 1980s pay less than $7,400 a year, which is 35 percent less than the poverty-level income for a family of four."

So you may not have to pitch a job at McDonald's; they, Kmart, and other entry-level jobs will continue to abound. (And why shouldn't their business be good? People can't afford to eat at "real" restaurants, which are closing in droves, or to shop at middle-class department stores, which are shutting their doors in greater numbers than ever before.) But if you're looking for a well-paying job—be you secretary, sales manager, or self-employed—the rules of the game have changed for good.

No, you didn't always have to pitch. There were jobs for all Americans who wanted to work, promising a good wage for the high-school diplomate and a great one for the college grad. A professional degree virtually guaranteed an upper-middle-class lifestyle, an opulent one if it was from a top-drawer school. (When I graduated from Columbia in the late seventies, the utterly useless "placement office" offered only this advice: "Don't say a degree in French hasn't prepared you for anything. Companies will always want a Columbia man." And they were right: There was always some kind of shabby-genteel job in advertising or publishing that you could work at for a year or two before going to law or business school.)

But, as the saying goes, That was then; this is now. And these, my friends—if you haven't found it out already—are the times that try men's and women's souls. As the above citations make amply clear, there are more people than jobs today; the employment situation is rather like a game of musical chairs where the chairs outnumber the butts by three to one. If you think it's not a pretty picture, you're right.

And the situation isn't likely to change anytime soon. In fact, the most recently emerging phenomenon in the working world is the substitution of consultancies, freelance, and temporary work—all without such luxuries as health insurance and retirement plans, thank you very much—for what used to be full-time jobs. Indeed, Rifkin writes:

> *Professional employment is . . . becoming temporary. The* Executive News *reports that more than 125,000 professionals work as temps every day. . . . Temporary workers and outsourcing make up the bulk of today's contingent workforce.*

Or, in the unapologetic words of William Bridges *(Job Shift: How to Prosper in a World Without Jobs)*, "We will all have to learn new ways to work."

There you have it, folks: Whether you be clerical, administrative, or executive material, temporary employment is, increasingly, the order of the day. There are pluses (freedom, intellectual stimulation) and minuses (no health insurance, the possibility of being evicted from your apartment at any moment) associated with this kind of work; we'll discuss these later. But like it or not, life as a worker-for-hire is the wave of the future, and learning how to get this kind of work is something many of us are going to need to know. And this book will tell you how to find it—not just now, but throughout your working life. All you need to do is to find, time and time again, your Perfect Pitch.

This changing face of employment in America is, frankly, what really propelled me to write this book. As a career counselor and motivational speaker, I've been helping people find jobs and change careers for years; but only recently has the scourge of corporate downsizing produced so huge a field of talented, hard-working, *jobless* folks—people who, by personal choice or as victims of circumstance, needed to temp, consult, or freelance to pay the bills, men and women with superior skills and oceans of experience, but who are clueless as to how to market—how to *pitch*—their hard-earned wisdom and desire to work.

Then there's the growing segment of workers who, by dint of their chosen careers, are going to have to pitch—themselves, their skills, their ideas—nearly every day of their lives. Actors, writers, small business owners, salespeople, lawyers, people whose jobs are virtually defined by their presentation of ideas, day in and day out. People like my friend Martin Sokol, one of Hollywood's most innovative and hottest young producers, who, despite his success, confided, "Really, Dave, I'm just winging it. I have to pitch several times a day, but I could use some tips as to organization, technique, and approach." It's for mavericks like Marty, committed job seekers, and the hundreds of thousands of men and women downsized by corporate greed that I write this book.

And, oh, by the way: If you're sitting smugly thinking you're above all this; that is, if you have a steady job, don't be quite so smug (though chances are, there aren't too many of you out there—studies show over half of all Americans are worried about losing their jobs). In today's supercompetitive employment climate, where jobs are stripped of protective corporate layers and people routinely perform the work of two former staffers, there's no such thing as deadwood: Everyone must pull his or her own weight. Accordingly, one thing I'll teach you in this book is ways you can pitch to keep your own job, subtle techniques that help keep you ahead of the pack.

So now that we're agreed that we all have to pitch, regardless of what we do and where we are, let's return to the first part of the question, namely, What Is a Pitch? In its most simple terms, stripped of all linguistic gobbledygook:

> *Pitching is about getting information across to a target audience in the clearest, most concise, and winningest possible way. Your Perfect Pitch is the one that makes your audience—whoever, whatever, and wherever they are—shout "Yes!"*

In other words, pitching is all about getting what you want by convincing your audience that what you're pitching (be it an idea, a concept, yourself) is something he or she just can't live without.

Without a doubt, the question most often asked of me is this: What is the difference between pitching and selling? It's a valid, even vital question whose answer, in effect, underscores the rai-son d'être of this book.

According to Webster's, to sell is "to impose upon . . . to deliver or give up in violation of duty, trust or loyalty" and even (egads!) "to betray." It is any wonder that used-car salespeople have such bad reps?

Pitching, on the other hand, is about communicating. If selling is talking *at* someone, pitching is talking *to*—and *with*—them. Selling is ultimately an act of narcissism; conversely, by explaining why a proposition is of use to all parties involved, pitching is an essentially humanistic skill.

Or think of it this way: Selling is tantamount to Stone Age Man clubbing his intended and dragging her back to his cave. Pitching is debonair Marcello Mastroianni doing his suave Latin lover routine in those *la dolce vita* films. It's the difference be-tween being wonked and wooed, between stealing and seduc-tion.

Still not sure why you need to pitch? Well, let me put it to you this way: If you don't pitch, someone else will. Statistics don't lie, and if your life has been untouched by downsizing and retrenchment, you're a lucky duck indeed. Lifetime employ-ment is a thing of the past; more and more of us will be working on a contingency basis or running our own businesses. Whether you're a laborer, foreman, or head of the firm, your lot in life is by no means guaranteed. "Good enough" no longer is, and, even if you're great, you're going to have to let other people know—not once in a while or when you think about it, but all the time.

This book will show you how to do just that: how to use pitching to get what you want out of your career, your job, your life. Pitching to win is a formula you'll use not just now, but always. And this is where you'll start.

3
...

What Can I Pitch?

First and foremost, you're going to be pitching yourself—the unique blend of talents and abilities only you have—today, tomorrow, and for the rest of your life. Whether you're actively seeking work or want to stay one step ahead of the game where you are now, you'll seize upon every possible opportunity to make your voice heard.

More specifically, you can pitch:

1. A job
2. A freelance assignment
3. A service you provide
4. A project you want to spearhead at work
5. An idea
6. A product
7. Your own business
8. Girl Scout cookies

Did the last item get your attention? Good. Then consider this:

Just yesterday, in the parking lot of my local supermarket, I was approached by a seven-year-old girl named LaKeisha.

"Mister, would you like to buy some Girl Scout cookies?"

"Oh, I'd love to, but they're too fattening."

"Sir, I don't think you have anything to worry about!"

"Well, aren't you a sweetheart! Okay, I'll take a box of the mint chocolate."

"Only one box? Mister, you know you're going to eat a whole box tonight."

(She had a point. Who doesn't devour an entire box of mint chocolate Girl Scout cookies in one sitting? LaKeisha knew her product like the back of her hand.)

"Okay, I'll take two."

"Great." (Cocking her head and directing her big brown eyes right at me.) "But, you know, if you bought three boxes, you'd help me achieve my goal for the night."

"What's your goal?"

"To sell more than anyone else!"

Am I a pushover, a nice guy, or had LaKeisha found her Perfect Pitch? A little bit of all three, I think. Anyway, I told LaKeisha I was writing a book about selling (to simplify matters) and that I was going to put her in it.

"Mommy, I'm going to be famous!" she trilled. Of that I have no doubt: I fully expect to see LaKeisha running for President in about thirty years. She knew how to pitch to get exactly what she wanted, and soon you will, too.

4
· · ·

Necessity Is the Mother of Invention or How I Learned to Pitch

Despite the fact that she can't act, delivers lines as if English weren't her native language, and has a mug that would make anyone in Brooklyn shout "*Mieskheit!*", Tori Spelling will never have to pitch.

Nor will John-John Kennedy (hell, it might have taken him three times to pass the bar exam, but with his combination of looks and connections, who cares?). And when Princess Stephanie of Monaco wanted careers as a recording artist and a swimwear designer (dalliances she gave up as fast as they came to her), all Daddy had to do was make a few quick calls.

But for most of us—and I'm talking 99 percent of humanity—who were born with neither superior family connections nor the face of Christy Turlington, selling ourselves is the name of the game. I'm not talking about pitching once, twice, or even thrice, but about incorporating the skill of pitching so thoroughly into our daily existence that it becomes an automatic reflex, an ongoing MO.

This I guarantee you: Once you get the hang of pitching—a job here, a project there, your achievements to your boss and beyond—it will come as naturally as getting up in the morning and brushing your teeth. Whether you work as a writer, actor, or small business head (the kinds of careers where pitching isn't elective, but key) or in the corporate world, the art of the pitch will become an almost involuntary part of your daily personal and professional lives.

So how did I become such a pitching pro? Very simple: I *had* to.

In high school, I was smart but too freaky to be the apple of my teachers' eyes; they had no idea what to make of our bohemian clique, who clutched Joni Mitchell albums to our bosoms and lived our suburban lives as characters out of *Cabaret*. We tried to make the bar of a local bowling alley our private salon, but were thrown out on our asses real fast. (Nobody had to defile my locker: I beat them to it, writing our slogan, *Divine Decadence!* on it before anybody could write something worse.) My artsy friends and I were kept out of the National Honor Society (when all the cheerleaders were let in) until the end of senior year, when the powers-that-be decided that if we were good enough for the Ivies, Montgomery Blair High School had better let us in the NHS.

The moral of the story is this: Despite being smart and hardworking, I was never a Golden Boy, and I knew, moreover, that I never would be. If I wanted to achieve anything in life, I'd have to fight for it tooth and nail; I'd have to pitch my persona and abilities as something better than people thought they were.

I can honestly say that my college applications served as the launch pad for a lifetime practice of pitching technique. Oh, I'd never have called it pitching then, but somehow I knew instinctively that to get into a great college, I'd have to do more than send in an application along with fifteen bucks. I'd even reinvent myself if required. In those days (the dark ages of the seventies!), we didn't have access to the myriad professional services whose sole function is to engineer high school seniors' acceptance to the college of their choice, and I thought Stanley Kaplan was my friend Ben's uncle! It was up to the individual boy or girl to sink or swim in the competitive waters of college admissions.

The cardinal rule of pitching is to know your audience, and to select targets where your pitch makes most sense. (It isn't always necessary, as a great pitch can overcome an intrinsically misguided target selection, but take it from someone who's spent too much time swimming up the wrong stream: Do yourself a favor, and make a good match.)

Aided by my high school's previous graduating class's recommendations and research (never turn up your nose at the chance to make life easier!), I deduced that Chicago and Columbia were the only places that would be even vaguely hospitable to someone like me; in fact, at these bastions of bohemian intellectualism, I might even be considered normal—an epithet that had never been ascribed to me at any time during the previous seventeen years. (Well, maybe Berkeley would've been okay, but that was too California, and Oberlin was too, well, Ohio. I wanted to hang out with Laura Nyro on fire escapes on the Upper West Side of Manhattan—little did I know.)

I was relatively unworried about Chicago—how many applicants with my grades and test scores did they have from

Maryland, after all?—or the other schools to which I applied. Columbia was where I wanted to go, so I put all my eggs in that basket. But—and here's the clincher—I made sure those eggs were the biggest, most beautiful ones the admissions office in Morningside Heights had ever seen.

So my work was cut out for me; my reinvention began. I knew *prima facie* that I had to present myself to the admission committee in a unique, appealing, even unassailably attractive light. And that's precisely what I proceeded to do.

The first thing I did was to make sure I knew everything possible about Columbia College. (Guess what? Knowing your target audience—its own special wants and needs—is a prime component of the Perfect Pitch; but we'll get to that soon.) So I reviewed the mountains of literature, considered it carefully with my own goals and talents in mind, and pulled out the following facts:

- Biology, English, and economics were popular majors, but only seven graduating seniors majored in French.
- Their French Department (which I knew to be among the nation's best) seemed heavily slanted toward twentieth-century writers and critical theory.
- About fifty percent of courses were required (including the ultimate tribute to Dead White Males, "Contemporary Civilization," a literary and philosophical kick line of the great minds of Western culture).

These vital stats amassed, what do you think I did? You got it (see how easy pitching is once you get the hang of it?): I spewed these facts right back at the admissions folks in my essays (how embarrassed would we be if we read those infamous essays ten or more years later? I can only hope mine have been shredded by some ersatz Fawn Hall!) and, equally importantly, my "on-campus interview." I gushed and spewed about how:

- only Columbia, with its esteemed Sartrian scholars, could sate my burning desire for existential erudition (knowing full well they'd be especially happy to welcome another French major, apparently an item of great arcana if not endangered-species status);
- the Contemporary Civilization coursework was especially attractive to me (given my lack of such classes in high school);
- of course, I just had to go to college in New York.

I was pitching, to be sure; happily, my stance was abetted by the fact that all of the above was true. (Especially the last point: If I didn't get the chance to rub shoulders with Laura personally, I at least knew from reading *Interview* magazine the name of the East Village club where David Bowie hung out, and where to find Patti Smith.) The bottom line: *I told the Columbia admissions committee what they wanted to hear.*

Most people, on the other hand, do just the opposite: They tell people what they, not their audience, feel, think, and want to hear. And they do nothing to point out their unique combination of skills and talents that have the ability to set them apart from the rest of the field, while consciously matching their own attributes to those of the target.

Case in point: If you're a water polo power, tell UCLA or USC how much you can add to their team; Carleton College in Minnesota, though a fine institution, couldn't care less. *Before pitching—to a school, employer, or potential customer—make sure you have what they want.* You might be fabulous enough to pitch snow to an Eskimo, but why bother?

I can remember one other important pitch I made in my college life. One of Columbia's peach work-study positions was as a publicity assistant in the public relations office of the Engineering School. Unlike most on-campus jobs, it was something you could actually put on your résumé; for those of us who aspired to write, it was even sweeter because the head of the office was a professor at Columbia's justly idolized Journalism School. I wanted that job, and bad!

So did about sixty other undergraduates. I made the first cut and was selected to interview with Kenneth Goldstein, the professor and PR head. Eventually, the age-old question was raised: "So what makes you the right person for this job?"

Now, most people, when hearing this question, freeze up fast. Wrong move. From this point onward, I command you that the only acceptable reaction to this eternal query is to *rejoice.* Why? Because you're in the driver's seat: The other person has stopped talking long enough for you to make your pitch. The time to knock 'em dead is *now.* To wit:

"Well, Professor Goldstein, let me ask you this: How many of the applicants for this job are working journalists?"

"None, of course; they're all in school."

"None except me: I'm the music columnist for the *Spectator* [Columbia's student newspaper], and I deal with industry publicists all the time. So I think I've learned a thing or two about the publicity game. That, along with my writing skills, would let me make great contributions to the engineering program's press efforts, don't you think?"

Well, apparently, he did think: I got the job, and kept it on my résumé for many years. (Unlike dredging up beers at the Rathskeller or working as a prostitute or bookie—something many collegians do, if you can believe all the books on these subjects—this helped me not only in the immediate time frame, but in the long run as well.) Maybe I needed the money more than the other applicants—and I certainly wanted the experience—but it was the packaging of my skills that made me the chosen one. I wouldn't have called it this then, but this much is clear: I had found my Perfect Pitch.

And it's a lesson I took to heart, and have used successfully time after time in my professional career. (You'll see bona fide examples as they occur throughout this book—my experiences, plus the case histories of clients and friends.) For now, I think you "get it": how pitching, and pitching alone, can make the difference between a near miss and the job or project of your dreams.

With that in mind, let's jump into the thick of things.

5
. . .

Seven Steps to a
Perfect Pitch

"All right," I hear you say (tapping your fingers impatiently), "I'm convinced. I know *why* I need to pitch and what kinds of things I can pitch; now tell me *how* to pitch."

With pleasure! Real-life examples are always the best, and this one is (as O.J. would say) "absolutely, 100 percent true." It's all about how I got my first break in the publishing world, and about how I could never have done it without finding—or at least, in my first uncertain steps, stumbling upon—my own Perfect Pitch. (By the way, don't worry that this isn't about finding a "real" job on-staff; there'll be plenty of examples of that to come. Freelancers and consultants, to whom I devote an entire chapter, will want to pay special attention here!)

About ten years ago, breaking temporarily free from the trenches of eyeshadow warfare at Revlon, I took a vacation in Spain, where I had taken along a big-name travel book. You know the kind—one of the big guns all the bookstores carry, full of statues, museums, and tourist-infested restaurants, but sadly devoid of the "inside" tips a young traveler really wants to know.

So I decided then and there that my life's mission was to write the best, coolest travel guide ever, one full of the kinds of information my friends and I would want to read, one containing the most "in" restaurants, coolest clubs, and trendiest hotels. Of course, my dream was tempered by the fact that I hadn't a clue as to how to proceed.

But I did some research—something that, as I stress ad nauseam, is key to every great pitch. Knowing the competition and your target is absolutely vital and thus became my first order of business, so I scoped out bookstores galore and deduced there was nothing even close to what I'd envisioned then on the shelves.

Okay, I had a great idea—now what? I did some more research at my local bookseller's, where I discovered a volume all about how to sell an idea for a book. Quickly I learned that in today's market one doesn't just send an outline to a publishing house; though this can result in book sales, 95 percent of books are sold via a literary agent. So I had to get me one of those; happily, the book I bought contained what appeared to be an exhaustive list of New York agents, along with their specialties.

In my mind, I was convinced that this was a great idea, and, workhorse that I am, I wrote a letter and prepared the mailing the very same day. My work ethic was admirable, but I made one important strategic mistake: In my zeal, I had failed to consider how to convince literary agents—my target audience—why the idea for this book was so good. Here's the letter I wrote:

Ms. Zelda Bookish
Literary Pretensions, Inc.
111 East 72nd Street, #3A
New York, NY 10022

Dear Ms. Bookish:

I've never written a book before, but have a great idea for one, so I hope you'll consider this proposal.

Recently, I was traveling in Europe and brought a mass-market travel guide along. Unfortunately, in the areas of greatest interest to me, I found the book sadly lacking.

So here's my idea: to write a really "with-it" guide for hip young people. It would be more akin to articles in trendy magazines than a typical travel book.

Please call me and let me know what you think. I'll be looking forward to hearing from you.

Sincerely,

David Andrusia

Hello! Not only is this letter as flat as a day-old Pepsi, but it's self-deprecating and vague. In fact, it breaks just about every rule of the Perfect Pitch. Like many others before me, I'd come up with a good idea but didn't know how to put it across to my target with precision and verve.

And where did it get me? Absolutely nowhere (unless you consider a pile of rejection letters a suitable consolation prize). With good reason, too: The letter contained an entirely weak pitch that ended up sounding more like a beggar's plea.

I may have been green (and pitchless!), but I wasn't ready to give up yet. So it was back to the drawing board (or, more precisely, typewriter—am I dating myself?), where I gave my idea—and how to pitch it—a lot more thought.

What I discovered was that my letter—my pitch—was grossly

inadequate. Not only did it fail to state a real point of difference, it barely communicated what my project was all about. I knew the book I wanted to write, but had not successfully communicated it—I hadn't *pitched* it—to my audience at all.

So I sat down with a pad and pencil and listed the most salient elements of my pitch:

1. Market demographics: Who would buy the book?
2. Uniqueness of slant/contents
3. My highly specific qualifications
4. Why readers would have to buy the book: counter objections
5. Writing samples to close the deal

With that in mind, I took pen to paper and redrafted the pitch as follows:

Dear Ms. Bookish:

80 percent of people over 35 buy guidebooks before traveling abroad . . . but only 23 percent of those aged 18 to 35 do!

Why? According to a survey by *Travel Week* Magazine, it's because they can't find a guidebook they really want to own.

But now they can! Enclosed is my proposal for a unique guide whose time has truly come: *EUROPE HOT AND HIP*. Among the information the reader will find nowhere else:

- RAVE RESTAURANTS, as only local groovesters know

- HAPPENING HOTELS, from superexpensive to dirt-cheap
- COOL CLUBS—the trendy/underground ones tourists never find on their own

Plus much, much more.

So why me? As a contributor to *Interview, Details, In Fashion,* and other "hip" publications, I have my finger on the pulse of what's happening. (Of course, even though I've done travel pieces for these magazines, people will still want to buy this book—how many of us really save clippings?) What's more, as a frequent traveler who speaks six languages, I find the best of the best like no ordinary travel writer can.

One last thing: As you probably know, travel books are among the top five sales categories of every bookstore in the United States. So a successful guide stands to do well in terms of royalties for us both.

I dare you to read my sample chapter on Madrid and not laugh out loud. Is this book a winner, or what?

Looking forward to your thoughts . . .

Happy trails!

David Andrusia

Before proceeding, I polished one last—and vital—part of my pitch: the target. The first time around, I let my enthusiasm get the better of me, and broadcast my pitch to virtually the entire universe of New York literary agents. (A great attitude and belief in yourself are essential, of course, and it's easy to think the whole world wants to know about our gifts. *Broadcasting* your pitch is of prime importance; *airing it selectively* can, at times, be even more so.) This time out, I decided to write first only to those agents who had actually included travel books in their agency roundup—that is, those who actually listed titles, not just an ostensible specialty in the travel book field. By doing the research every great pitch requires—and, consequently, airing my pitch to just the right audience—I was honing in on my Perfect Pitch.

Of course, you've already guessed the end of the story: I found an interested agent who, in turn, pitched the book successfully to a major publishing house. The book was published, was named "Europe's hippest guide" by no less than *Vogue* magazine, and started me on my book writing career.

What was the difference between the two letters? Let's consider this via my proven pitching technique.

Seven Steps to a Perfect Pitch

1. Define Goal

What are you pitching? Say it as pithily as possible—in ten words or less is best.

Here: A never-before-seen travel book.

2. Be Clear

Leave no room for misinterpretation of your major selling points or principal point of difference.

Here: I stressed the specific kinds of information to be included in my book.

3. Be Specific

After you've stated your initial proposition, be sure to provide the specifics—the features that figure most prominently in making your pitch unique.

Here: I included a blow-by-blow overview of exactly what would be in the guide: restaurants, hotels, clubs, etc.

4. Provide Proof

Don't leave your audience guessing: Tell them exactly why you can do what you say—and provide concrete examples to support your claims.

Here: By providing market demographics, I made the strongest case of all. (Facts are always more potent than mere feelings, which are insupportable and thus unconvincing at best.)

5. Be Unique

Reinforce the fact that you can provide something no one else can; restate your primary point of difference.

Here: I gave a full market survey that showed conclusively that no other guide could fit this bill.

6. Counter Objections

Shoot down potential objections even before they occur; this is the champion pitcher's stock-in-trade.

Here: I knew prospective editors would think magazines might already be doing similar stories—so I nipped the objection in the bud by explaining why this wasn't the case (i.e., why people would still need to buy my book).

7. Seal the Deal

Don't leave anything to chance; make sure you're always in the driver's seat. Successful pitches always put the pitcher in an active, not passive, position.

Here: I offered a dare, and included a sample chapter that I believed would sell the book. Testimonials, facts, proof—whatever is appropriate—work wonders that mere words never can.

6
...

Creating Your Personal Perfect Pitch: A Step-by-Step Guide

There's just one small step standing between you and your Perfect Pitch: knowing what you're pitching and to whom you're going to pitch it.

Laughing yet? You won't be for long. Yes, I fully realize that the above statement is simple and (it would seem) obvious enough to be, as Dieter on *Saturday Night Live* would have it, "at once vapid and jejune." But your guffawing should come to an abrupt stop when I tell you that as many as 90 percent of my clients can't answer this entirely straightforward question in a concise and cogent way.

And I'm not talking about normally confused minds. I'm here to tell you that polished, purebred professionals in all fields of endeavor begin mumbling like simpletons when I put this question to them. As a matter of fact, the higher up the career ladder you go, the more jumbled and incoherent the answer usually is.

There are a couple of reasons for this. The first, to my mind, is that the more accomplished a person is, the less he or she thinks a strategic job-changing plan applies to them. I've got a wonderful education and career thus far, this category of individual thinks, and I know people will be coming to me with all kinds of fabulous offers. Yeah, right—and I'm marrying Lisa Marie Presley tomorrow night.

(The important caveat to the above, however, is that once you start using my techniques of the perfect self-promotional pitches I discuss later, your visibility in your industry can increase exponentially. And, once you're seen as a "player," folks well may come after you. But that's jumping ever so slightly ahead of the game.)

The second reason people fail to devise a solid plan of action is six letters long: D-E-N-I-A-L. The words *fired, laid off,* and even the gorgeous British euphemism *redundant* cut like a knife. Like their romantic equivalents, *jilted, dropped,* or the piercingly hateful *rejected,* these are words too painful even to contemplate. So we run around like ostriches, somehow using the most advanced defense mechanisms in the arsenal of the human psyche to convince ourselves it just isn't true. We're not unemployed; we're "on a hiatus," "on sabbatical," or "taking a breathing spell."

As if! And I know, chickadees, 'cuz I been there myself. "What, me—unemployed? Not in this lifetime, buddy!" We curse our bosses, our luck, our lives, then hurriedly bury the memory of our last job like a body that's still alive. (Too bad we couldn't bury our *boss's* body, right?)

And then we call a few friends and colleagues for referrals (thinking this halfhearted effort represents the "networking" we hear so much about), send a few résumés to employment agencies and headhunters, answer a few ads, and wait for the phone to ring. And wait and wait and wait.

In those lazy, hazy days of early unemployment, we mentally recite all our favorite feel-good pop philosophies: "There's a reason for everything," "Out of crisis comes opportunity," and the vague, all-purpose "It's for the best." (Here, fill in the sunny greeting-card sentiment of your choice.) When not involved in our meager job-hunting efforts, we spend the remaining twenty-three hours of the day "doing things we always wanted to do": voice lessons (in southern California, at least, this is hands-down the number one answer), getting in shape (though experience shows that most out-of-work people are in much *worse* shape than they were before), taking classes (in L.A., pet psychic readings are all the rage), and (hold me while I gag) "getting in touch with our inner child." One acquaintance is actually undergoing an advanced seminar in "rebirthing." (What is it? Damned if I know, but I sure don't want to be there when the water breaks.)

After a few months of trying to be the next Alanis Morissette and still not having a clue as to what Fluffy is *really* thinking, we start to get peeved, but—no worries!—as the song title goes, "Things're Gonna Work Out Fine." So we take a few more classes, think a little bit more about working out, and take the vacation we never had time for when we were working. And, oh yes, if we happen to be running short of dough we send out a few more résumés and make a few more desultory calls.

Because, after all, we know in our hearts that the universe will take care of us and the job of our dreams is just a phone call away. (And so is Fabio, with a plate of real butter in hand.)

Yes, this is just a temporary setback that will, in time, resolve itself. Like the Greek tragedians of yore, we're all waiting for that deus ex machina that sweeps us up and delivers us from all our cares. (As one wayward client of mine whom I ran into at a coffee house in a cappuccino semi-overdose put it: "I guess I didn't do what you told me to because it just all seemed like too much work, and I'm still thinking some headhunter is going to call me tomorrow with a fabulous job." Nearly a year later? I don't think so!)

And that's the bad news: Using my techniques of the Perfect Pitch requires *work*. Any job hunting does, of course, but mine requires even more. What's more, this is work for which you'll not be immediately paid, which is why many people end up in jobs they really don't want—or worse yet, in a coffee house surrounded by empty cappuccino vats.

Now, here's the good news: By exerting the extra effort my program requires, you will be able not only to get a job faster and quicker, but you can actually guide yourself into the job of your dreams, whether you're currently working, unemployed, just starting out, or looking to change the direction of your career. There's even a chapter on pitching for freelancers and consultants—whether you're in this role due to downsizing or your own personal choice.

Even better news: When you decide how you're going to position yourself and where you're going to look, you're already halfway home. Many of my clients are surprised when I tell them this, but it's true. Of course, there's a fair degree of soul-searching and roll-up-your-sleeves research between here and there, but once you get to that pretty point, the rest of your search is a relative breeze. And to quote the fabu Staple Singers pop/gospel classic, "I'll Take You There." Here's how:

Developing Your Personal Perfect Pitch

In developing your own Perfect Pitch, it's always helpful to keep in mind those four journalistic guideposts: who, what, when, and where. The bottom line: When you've answered all these questions to the best of your ability, your preliminary work is done.

Let's take care of the easy one first.

The Perfect Time:
When Should I Pitch?

If you've got a trust fund, a rich spouse, or are living in someone's garage, circle the song-title answer of your choice:

(a) "You Oughta Know"

(b) "Tomorrow"

(c) "The Last Time I Saw Paris"

(d) "Whenever I Call You Friend"

For everyone else—and I'm presuming that includes you, since you bought (or shoplifted) this book—the only possible answer is this: "Immediately." (Good. Now we've got the no-brainer out of the way.)

The Perfect Pitch:
What Am I Going to Pitch?

First and foremost, you're pitching yourself. But as what, and to whom? Even for the most seasoned workers, these questions are far less obvious than you'd think. From recent graduates to pros with decades of experience, the stuttering and stammering begins as soon as these queries leave my tongue.

Among the least favorable replies:

- "Something in the health-care industry."
- "A job working with people."
- "The military?"
- "In the food industry."

If your answer falls into this range, I must be totally honest and tell you that you've bought the wrong book. Certainly, I could help you in a series of one-on-one career counseling sessions, but it's beyond the scope of this (or any) book to tell you whether your parachute is blue, green, or red.

Miles better, but still nowhere near a Perfect Pitch, are job objectives like these:

- Nurse
- Chef
- Accounting
- Finance executive
- Model booker
- Writer
- Gardener
- Anthropologist

In candor, I breathe a sigh of relief when clients come to me with an occupation, no matter how general, because stratifying and streamlining their pitch is child's play from then on in.

The Perfect Target: Who, What, and Where Am I Going to Pitch?

So you're a gardener—groovy. But what kind of gardener? Specifically:

(a) *What* is your specialty and affinity: large public grounds, private homes; what kind of plants do you know best?

(b) *Where* do you want to garden? Chicago? Cook County? Anywhere in Illinois? The entire Midwest?

(c) *When* can you work? (For most of humanity, as mentioned above, we need work all the time; thus, this is always the least important question of the group.)

(d) *Why* are you the best gardener who ever lived? What is your personal Perfect Pitch?

Similarly, you can't just be "in marketing." You've got to develop a far more specific target—the logistical end—before you can further delineate your most Perfect Pitch. In short, you've got to be:

A seasoned packaged goods marketer looking for a position as group product manager with a blue-chip grocery products manufacturer . . . a University of Texas MBA who combines classic product management skills with new product development prowess of the first rank.

Or, in the former example:

A gardener with twenty years' experience in all phases of private property landscaping, with special focus on flowering plants, who is looking for new clients in northern Illinois.

Before you can state your target as clearly and concisely as this, do not pass Go. (Just turn to page 154 and consider the case of Jodie, whose nebulous goal was "something in writing" to see exactly what I mean.)

Now, let's consider a couple of finite examples in two widely different fields to make this point clearer still:

Perfect Pitch #1: Matthew

When Matthew signed up as a client, he was already near the top of the heap. Far from floundering, he made a fine income as a staff accountant with a Big Eight firm. So when I asked him what he wanted, I was dismayed to hear the following all-too-frequent response: "I want to stay in accounting."

(Well, like, duh.) "That's good," I replied, "because with a face like that, you're not going to give Denzel Washington a run for his money." (Matthew was very handsome, or I wouldn't have made this crack!) "What kind of accounting, Matt?"

"Um, well, I'm not really sure. I just feel really thwarted in what I'm doing now. But I do love accounting, and I have no desire to leave the field."

"Well, you're a CPA working for one of the most prestigious accounting firms in the nation. What's not to like? Is it the size of the firm, or something else?"

"No, it's not that. To be honest, I like the salary and prestige of working for a Big Eight; in our field, it's the ultimate wet dream."

"Oh, really? I thought Claudia Schiffer was more your type."

"Touché. But seriously, I like working for a big, fancy firm."

"So what's the problem?"

"Well, it's hard to say. Okay, one problem is definitely my boss. He's the biggest asshole who ever walked the face of the earth."

"Most bosses are; it's in their job descriptions. Next?"

"Oh, boy. Um . . . okay. I have to tell you that I think I've been at the same level too long and I should be one step ahead. Don't get the impression that I'm falling behind or doing badly—I just don't think I'm on the fast track, and maybe one way to get there is to change companies."

"That's a valid concern, and sometimes going to a new company can help achieve that goal. So would you say that you want to target only Big Eight firms?"

"Well, mainly, but I'm not averse to expanding my horizons. I mean, if I stay in corporate accounting, I definitely want to stay in the Big Eight, if only because I can. But [sheepishly] there's kind of another area I want to explore. . . ."

"Namely?"

"I know you're going to laugh, but I've always dreamed of working in advertising."

"Why would I laugh? It's an exciting field, and Chicago is a major regional capital in the advertising game."

"I know, but it sounds so . . . so flimsy. Like I just want to do it to be in a glamour field."

"No, Matt, dancing on tabletops is, as you put it, flimsy. Working as an accounting executive in an advertising agency is hardly a shadowy job."

(Laughing) "Yeah, I know. But I keep thinking, 'If I left a Big Eight firm, what would other people think?' "

"Listen, my friend, starting today you have two choices in life: Doing what makes Matt happy and doing what you think other people would like. And, besides," I continued, grinning, "I hate to burst your bubble, but your in-the-closet advertising target isn't exactly the most bohemian lifestyle choice I've ever heard. I don't think anyone would be shocked by such a job, unless you decided to do it in drag."

Matt lowered his eyes and scratched his chin. "Well, maybe I could do that . . . is that what you mean by a Perfect Pitch?" (Then cracking up . . .)

"Now, let's not get carried away. Although that would be a pitch, maybe in this case it wouldn't be the perfect one—though you'd be a shoo-in for Oprah's next show on corporate transvestites. Okay, Matt, enough clowning around. We really are getting somewhere. When you walked into my office, you wanted to do 'something in accounting.' Now we've already refined that to two main goals: (1) a senior staff position with a Big Eight accounting firm, and (2) a financial management position with a major advertising agency. So the next question is this, Matt: Where?"

"Oh, only in Chicago, David. My roots, my whole life, is there. One thing I know is I've no desire to move."

"Well, in one sense, that makes our job easier, because you've got a very circumscribed universe in which to work. On the other, it's harder, because the range of options is much more limited than if you were willing to consider even a slightly expanded geographical area, say Milwaukee and Detroit, which you may want to do once you see how many targets there are in the Chicago metropolitan area alone."

"Hmm. Tell you what: let's see what's in Chicago and go from there."

With this goal, the following target strategy came into view:

Geographical Target: Chicago

Big Eight accounting firms	8
Major advertising agencies	20

It's obvious that, given Matt's very finite target area, the number of target employers is fairly small. Of course, there's an upside, which is this: A Big Eight accounting firm employs scores of accountants, so the total number of opportunities for one with a strong, "like" background is much greater than one per company; in fact, if Matt writes to, say, five vice presidents (or senior vice presidents, depending on the corporate structure) at each firm, he has already expanded the total number of pitch targets from one to five. (Note: Compare this to someone pitching to companies that only employ one person in their field. A hair salon, for example, will have at the most one manicurist working there; a manicurist applying to a shop that does only nails will have a five- or six-time better chance there—and would thus have to contact fewer nail parlors than hair salons, if the laws of probability hold true.)

Researching Target Employers

In most cases, defining the kinds and locations of organizations you'd like to work for is the easy part. Much harder and more research intensive is finding out where they are, and whom you should write to there.

Happily, there are reference works listing organizations in almost any imaginable field—from aerospace to performing arts, and everything else in between. If you're still in school, ask your career placement officer to point you toward the guides that are right for you.

If you're in the working world you should already know where to turn, whether you're a year out of school or the proverbial old hand. (Part of your lifetime Perfect Pitch is always keeping your finger on the pulse of what's happening in your field.) If you're still baffled, you should:

(a) Call colleagues in your field and ask if they know where a categorical directory can be found.

(b) Call the industry trade association(s) in your field. (Almost every occupational category has at least one.)

(c) Call the advertising department of your industry's top trade publication(s). If you're a big wheel, they'll probably pass a mailing list on for free; if not, they'll probably ask you to pay for these names, but it's worth it as a last resort.

(d) Refer to the appendix at the back of this book for a list of reference guides in major industries and professional categories.

For people in the business world, the hands-down favorite reference is the *Standard Directory of Advertisers,* more commonly known as the *Red Book.* All business libraries and many general branches have this guide, but beware: With budget cuts, many libraries will have reference books that are years old. Talk to the reference librarian and make sure the guide you're using—whatever your target occupation—is the most recently published one. (If you live in a rural or exurban setting and this necessitates a day trip, by all means do whatever is necessary to spend time on the road. Most of these publications are superexpensive, and it's worth the price of gas or busfare to do this very necessary research.)

Important Note: Whatever your profession and whatever the guide, don't take the names and titles given as the final word. Even if the directory you're using has the current calendar year printed on its spine, the information contained within is (at the least) several months old. Certainly, if yours is a high-mass mailing (hundreds of names long), you'll not have the time or resources to call each name, but do verify the names and positions of companies that are high on your target list.

How many calls does this entail? There's no hard-and-fast rule; the answer depends on how much you want to work for that company and how much time you have. *Big Tip:* While, as I note later on (see page 81), you should mark "Private" or "Personal" on highly targeted letters, don't do so for mass mailings unless you definitely know that person is still with the firm. This is because if you mark "Private" and the person is no longer with the firm, the letter will be forwarded (or worse, deposited at a dead-letter office). On the other hand, if "Private" isn't marked on the letter and you address it to a "Lois Katz, Vice President, Finance" who is no longer with the firm, Ms. Katz's successor will almost definitely take the bait. (Of course, it would be better to have the new VP's name on the envelope and letter, but a fabulous pitch letter won't go ignored even if you've made the blunder of not being up to date.)

Another Important Note: A key component of your lifetime Perfect Pitch is a Rolodex or computer file that's constantly updated; trust me that this will prove worth its weight in platinum. I myself have moved cross-country about a zillion times, and while I have no idea where my Blondie and X-Ray Spex records ended up, I've kept my Rolodex clutched to my bosom at all times. (Once there was a fire in my New York tenement and I ran down five flights with only my wallet and Rolo in hand!) *The mailing list you amass now isn't yesterday's news; rather, it's a permanent, valuable resource you should maintain throughout your career.*

How will you update this list? Later on, in the chapter on "sleuthing," you'll learn how careful perusal of trade publications, plus business periodicals (including the business section of your local newspaper), is a wellspring of information. Reading these with a special eye to staff changes is the best possible way to make sure the personal directory you're currently compiling remains super up to date. (I'm the first to admit I've sold my own lists in the toy, cosmetics, and entertainment industries for a pretty penny to friends and colleagues who were too lazy to do the research themselves.)

Now, back to Matt. As we've already seen, his target audience is fairly limited and confined to two major categories. But know this: It's precisely in instances where a search is so narrow (in this case, defined by geography and company type) that he has to squeeze every bit of juice out of each entry. Finding the addresses of the Big Eight accounting firms in Chicago is child's play; researching whom to write to at each is rather more complex.

This is also a perfect example of where, because of the circumscribed nature of Matt's search, it's vital he know that each person and title to whom he is writing is absolutely correct. Look at it this way: If you're the only person driving on a four-lane highway, you can veer over the line from time to time with no harm done; but if it's a crowded Autobahn packed with BMWs doing ninety, you'd better stay in your lane! In the speedway analogy and in Matt's search, the room for error is just about nil. If making forty calls is the only way to get this information, then forty calls he must make.

Now, how do you know whom to write to in a given company? In Matt's case, having worked for the same kind of firm, he was one step ahead of the game: He knew the general setup of a large accounting concern, and what title(s) he should contact at each place. (Note: When I say there are five senior VPs at each company, I'm doing so for argument's sake; in point of fact, one may have three and another eight. The accounting industry guide Matt uses will list each company's personnel roster separately.)

At this juncture, we must consider a highly salient point.

Personnel Departments: To Send or Not to Send?

"Personnel," "Human Resources," or "Staffing"; by any name, their function is the same. And, yet, depending on the company's size, outlook, and relative degree of sophistication, the difference among them can be night and day.

I know some personnel chiefs who have doctorates in organizational behavior, and others who just fell off the turnip truck. The degree of function and responsibility of departments from company to company varies so widely that no one in his or her right mind could possibly make a final decree as to their valor and worth—or, for that matter, how to approach them in an organization you're approaching as an outsider.

The truism is that executives (manager level and above) should pitch directly to the head of the department in which they want to work, and only clerical and administrative personnel should go through Personnel. Certainly, there's truth to this, but the following examples dispel this attitude as gospel.

1. Some—not many, but some—human resources directors (or VPs) are finely attuned not only to the corporate culture, but to its very workings, and can state with great precision not only what the job entails, but how it fits into the big picture. What this means: If these talented personnel executives get your résumé, they will do something with it—call you in, pass it on to key staff—even if you're not responding to an ad. There is thus every reason they should see your pitch and résumé.

The problem, of course, is that with the exception of personal recommendations, there's no way of knowing whether your target organization's personnel chief is ab fab or has simply been with the company one year less than God. The bottom line is this: If you're a professional (as opposed to clerical) worker, writing to a target firm's personnel head is much less efficacious than writing to the head of the department in which you want to work, but in the case of your top-twenty list, it probably couldn't hurt. Just don't expect too much, and you'll be fine.

But always remember this: The Personnel Department can only help you when you're applying for a job that's exactly like or incredibly similar to the job you have right now. Apples to apples, pears to pears. If you're careening headfirst into a new area or whole new field (good for you!), save the expense of phone and postage for a double-decker ice cream cone (or whatever is your favorite treat).

2. *Consider the case of Eliza (page 88), a secretary who pitched herself as a high-level executive aide.* She wrote directly to corporate heads, which reverses the standard view of clerical staff only being hired through Personnel.

• • •

So now Matt has his list of Big Eight accounting firm department heads. How to find the advertising agency names—and whom to write to there?

The first part is easy; there are legions of guides on the advertising industry, most of which list companies by size and some by region. A quick call to the Midwest edition of *Adweek* magazine would solve Matt's problem fast. (*Adweek* also publishes annual directories of ad agencies and advertisers that are among the very best—clear, concise, and easy to use.)

The second part is harder, and it's an inextricable part of his Perfect Pitch. Because he's changing fields slightly, he needs to pitch his guts out to key executives at the ad firms. (In this instance, apples to oranges, writing directly to Personnel would be a waste of good stationery and postage stamps.)

So far, so good. But now we're approaching virgin territory, unexplored ground, and the area that will make or break Matt's cross-company job campaign: his Perfect Pitch. We know that ad agencies employ accountants, but what exactly do they do, and how can Matt's experience be a unique asset to them?

Researching the first question isn't always easy—in fact, sometimes, as an outsider it's damned hard—but remember this: The onus is on you. If you're familiar with the inner workings of your target organization(s), breathe a sigh of relief; if not, it's your job to turn over every stone in search of the information that helps you answer the questions, What specific job(s) am I going after? And, How can I pitch myself to an organization in the winningest possible way?

When you elect to remain within the confines of a given career, the answer is usually quite clear. But when you're looking to make a move sideways, zigzag, or diagonally, even the clues are harder to find.

First, ask your friends. It's not a trade secret how an accountant or comptroller works within the body of an ad agency, and almost anyone working at a level above the mail room could tell you this in a flash. Nor do you need to know all the minutiae of that job; the broad strokes will do just fine.

Second, write for the company's annual report. It will give you an overview of what the company does, and how it seeks to differentiate itself from the competition. It won't divulge the whole story, of course, but there may well be select pearls from which you can devise a pitch responding to the company's apparent short- and long-term needs.

Third, trip on over to the big bookstore of your choice. It's a happy coincidence that almost every field—from the recording industry to construction—has a book devoted to it. (When I was just out of school, I read several, and they gave me a wonderful overview of the fields I was interested in.) Be persistent! Although bookstores tend to be better staffed than many retailers, don't accept "I don't know" as an answer to the question, "Do you have a book on the commercial fishing industry?" If the kid behind the counter looks stoned or bored, ask to speak to a manager. If they can't find what you're looking for (which they should, except in a really arcane or erudite field), ask them to consult *Books in Print,* the Bible of the publishing world. I'm not saying there's a book on every possible field, but there are on many, and they can be of enormous help.

So now our pal Matt has done his homework and knows what he's after: a position as comptroller or (in a super-sized ad firm) associate comptroller. (Most agencies also have a chief financial officer, but at the age of twenty-five, Matt's experience level was nowhere near that high.) And the most important part of that job was to monitor and oversee an agency's financial workings, from its owner expenditures in creative and administrative areas to the collection of billed funds. Matt's question—common to all Perfect Pitches—becomes this:

What do I have to offer this company—and how can I position (pitch) it to them in a manner that makes them shout "Yes!"?

Your goal here is always the same: to have a hiring authority prick up his or her ears, think you're the hottest thing since cream cheese, and want to see you even if no job currently exists.

Think that's impossible? Then think again. Here's why: In my whole career, I have never not seen an exceptional candidate, regardless of whether I had a job to offer when their résumé crossed my desk. That, I'm afraid, is because they are rarer than natural blondes.

Oh sure, I saw résumés that contained the names of great companies and fabulous schools, and as I said in the introduction, these are the people I would call in if I actually had a job to fill. But the people who wrote to tell me what they could do for me, why they should be at Company X—those sterling souls who took the time to *pitch*—were few and far between.

With this in mind, and his research done, it was time for Matt and me to plan his Perfect Pitch.

"Matt," I said, "you've done very well. I'm looking at a primary target list of about seventy names that was meticulously prepared. It's not the largest hit list I've ever seen, and in fact it's rather less than most of my clients' initial target mailings, but that's a function of your geographical restrictions. Nonetheless, it's a fine list."

"Well, thanks. I appreciate the positive feedback."

"You're welcome, sir. Now all we have to figure out is your Perfect Pitch."

"Right . . . but first I have a question."

"Fire away."

"I can fully understand why I need to pitch to the ad agencies, since what I'm doing now, though not unrelated, isn't a perfect fit. But do I really have to pitch to the accounting firms?

After all, I'm working for one of the country's most prestigious ones, and people go to other Big Eight companies all the time."

"That's a great question, and it's one I'm asked a lot. In total honesty, the short answer is no. If you're going from a square peg to a square peg, pitching isn't de rigueur. It's utterly conceivable that you could go from Company A to Company B by submitting a nondescript cover letter and 'just okay' résumé. But tell me this: Do you want a good job or a great one?"

"A great one, of course!"

"Then you can't be just another candidate; you have to be someone the company would feel crazy not to have. You have to find your Perfect Pitch."

"So you're saying I shouldn't send my résumé, just a pitch letter?"

"Here's the rule. With apples to apples, send a résumé, because your appropriateness for the position will be absolutely clear. In fact, having done almost exactly the same job will enhance your chances, especially in these downsized times when, all things being equal, most companies would rather not take any risks at all."

"But for the advertising agencies . . ."

"You guessed it: pitch, yes; résumé, no."

"Fine, but how will they know where I went to school?"

"You have to wear a college sweatshirt. It's a nonnegotiable part of the Perfect Pitch."

"Get out!"

"Matt, there isn't a law that says a cover letter can't include your educational credentials. But we'll get to that soon. First, we have to talk about more recent stuff—like what you've accomplished at your present firm, and what you can do for another one. Even more important, we have to discover what you have to offer to an ad agency."

"Well, David, I've thought about that because I know that's the ultimate angle of the Perfect Pitch. And here's the thing: I've never actually worked at an agency, so I can't give specific examples. Rather, I can paint a picture of how my present experience could work wonders on an agency's behalf."

"Perfect. What have you come up with?"

"This letter. What do you think?"

This is what I thought: that with some minor tweaking, Matt's letter was just about perfect. He observed all seven steps to the Perfect Pitch, and came out sounding like a candidate any ad firm would want to have. This is it:

> Mr. Jason Chase
> Chief Financial Officer
> CHASE & CHANG ADVERTISING
> 333 Wacker Drive
> Chicago, Ill 66666
>
> Dear Mr. Chase:
>
> To most people, accountants are just "number crunchers." Ay, but there's the rub: crunching those numbers just the right way can make the difference between a healthy company and financial disease.
>
> Case in point: my rescue operation for Marlow Manufacturing, one of my clients at Deloitte & Touche where I'm currently a senior staff accountant. After investigating the company's total financial picture, I discovered that it wasn't their sales alone that were lowering profit margins

by 30 percent; it was the firm's collections policies, uneven staffing arrangements, and out-of-line expense reports that were causing the crunch. After just six weeks as an accounting consultant, I began implementing changes that now—four months later—have already increased profits over last year by a remarkable 23 percent.

So why am I writing to you? Because now, after having earned a strong grounding at one of the company's most respected accounting firms, I'd like to turn my rescue talents to the industry of my choice: yours! Of course that's only natural, since I minored in marketing at New York University, where I earned (with honors) my undergraduate accounting degree.

I'll call soon to see if we can meet to discuss how my accounting wizardry can help make your agency the most profitable it's ever been.

Cordially,

Matthew Marnes

Has Matthew satisfied all seven conditions of the Perfect Pitch? You bet he has! He defined his goal (1); was clear and specific (2 and 3); provided proof (4); positioned his blend of skills and background as unique (5); countered objections in an attractive way by alluding to his marketing studies (6); and sealed the deal (7) by making a highly appealing proposition (to save the agency money—what could be a stronger pitch?) and putting himself in the driver's seat by telling Jason Chase to expect his call.

Here, a few pitch points need slight clarification:

1. *Change the level of your target hiring authority as the job and size of company changes.* In this case, Matt is writing to the chief financial officer because large companies have one; in a small-to-medium-sized firm, it would make more sense to write directly to the president of the firm.

2. *To call or not to call?* This is the age-old question, and the answer is entirely up to you because there's no hard-and-fast rule. More than anything else, it's a function of two issues: How big your target list is, and how attractive a prospective employer is relative to other organizations on your primary list. In Matt's case, I would call each and every one because he can't afford to miss this final chance to help seal the deal—in this case, to secure an interview with the addressee.

If, however, you're pitching by mail to over 1,000 names (which some of my out-of-work, financially precarious clients must do), you couldn't possibly call all 1,000, especially those organizations that are out of town. But you can and should call the top 50, 100, or 150 as a means of closing the first part of the deal, the interview itself. I can offer guidance here, but ultimately it's up to each client to decide for him- or herself.

3. *How many times should you call?* To quote Jacqueline Susann, "Once Is Not Enough." You may want to refer to my phone pitching techniques on page 181, but in general, be prepared to call three or four times. By then, you should have some feedback from the person's assistant (or not, if voice mail is involved) as to whether the person will take the time to see you; calling more than five times is both obnoxious and, to be blunt, beating a dead horse. Move on: There are bigger, friendlier fish to fry!

• • •

We've just seen how a personal pitching plan works for someone in the buttoned-down business world. Would this work as well for job seekers in other fields—teachers, illustrators, horse trainers? You already know, smart reader, that the answer is yes! Let's say it again, and say it loud:

Whatever the job, wherever you are, a strategic personal pitching plan is the cornerstone of your Perfect Pitch.

In the plainest of words: You can have the best damn pitch in the world, but if it isn't heard by all the right people in all the right places, it ain't worth dang. Whether you're a medical intern or mail room clerk, you must broadcast your interest—yes, pitch!—to the greatest number of potential employers within your geographic and professional base. Looking for a job or freelance gig is very much a numbers game, and the greater the number of targets you lay out, the greater the chance of a bull's-eye for you. (Read: a job.)

This is the perfect time to interject a very nineties kind of thought. Just as "any love is good lovin' " (or so the tacky power-pop song of the seventies went), I say that "any work is good workin' "—so cast your net as far, as wide, and as deep as it'll go. As recently as ten years ago, working for anything less than a blue-chip firm effected a chilly reception for top-drawer head-hunters and the employment elite. Today, with those firms re-trenching—or, at best, keeping staffing levels the same—they're virtual stagnant targets for job hunters in many fields. Of course, these firms should be prominent in your pitching plan, and, for many folks, the prestige (real or apparent) of working for a big name will never fade.

Fine for them—but don't let these big guns eclipse other

attractive targets in your field. If you read your daily newspaper religiously, you already know that in today's marketplace small-to-medium-sized organizations are the places where jobs at all levels are being created at a much higher rate than in the corporate behemoths of yore. The bottom line: Don't overlook small companies, where the jobs really are. Besides, if you're a go-getter with an entrepreneurial bent, I can guarantee you'll be happier making things happen and taking risks at a growing concern (and, probably, miserable at a corporate giant that moves at a snail's pace).

Wherever your targets, whatever size they are, you damn well better have a lot of them. In fact, the single biggest mistake my clients share is a pathetically small target base. Don't retract like a clam; expand your wings to butterfly length! (Okay, an eagle if you're the macho type.) And, as I tell friends and clients alike, don't *even* be givin' me no attitude when I say you haven't done nearly enough research. ("Another day at the library?" I've heard 'em moan. "Uh-huh," I answer. "Either that or another day of unemployment, baby. The choice is yours.")

Research is locating potential employers and finding out what they do so you can grace them with your Perfect Pitch.

Research is not parking your butt in front of the TV with a valu-bag of Mallomars listening to Jenny Jones discuss "Hermaphrodites: The More, the Merrier."

This problem—also known as laziness—is hardly confined to full-time job hunters; if anything, freelancers and consultants have it even worse. That's because, quite frankly, the range of options is greater, more research is required, and, most germane of all, pitching is a lifetime, not sporadic, thing. (This is precisely why I "read" clients in five minutes flat and advise all but the most intrepid against the freelance/consulting/small business route. Ninety percent of people don't have the gumption and get-up-and-go to make it on their own, and however miserable they may be in the on-staff world, I know they'll be even unhappier trying to procure work day after day. Even for the gutsiest guys and gals, the freelance life is rather like falling off a cliff; you better be fearless if you want to survive.) For more on pitching as a freelancer/consultant, Chapter 18 is your ultimate guide.

Perfect Pitch #2: Paula

I've shown you how Matt, an accountant, devised a perfect personal pitching plan by compiling the best possible—indeed, the most definitive—target list he could. While I think you've taken my admonitions to heart and understand why the most perfect possible hit list is so terribly key, let's go through this exercise one mo' time. And to drive home the point (if I haven't already driven it into the ground!) that this is true of workers in all fields, this example will be of the farthest thing from a business maven; we'll now cast our gaze on a not-for-profiteer.

Paula was calm, cool, and collected—just the way I like my clients. (It's a good thing I took a double-undergraduate major in psychology and buy Kleenex in bulk; consoling the jobless and petrified career-changers makes me just like Oprah, if a couple hundred million bucks poorer.) No, Paula swept in with all the composure and allure of Anjelica Huston in "The Grifters": She was looking for the next angle, and looking for it fast.

"I'll not waste your time, and I hope you'll not waste mine," she commanded in a crisp lockjaw. "I'm presently head of fund-raising for one of the country's major foundations, whose name I'd rather not disclose unless we elect to work together. Unfortunately, it appears that a major staffing change is imminent and I may be asked to leave. It is absolutely requisite that I locate a new position at my present or higher level in the shortest possible period of time. I am supporting two children, both of whom board at school, without the help of their father, for reasons I would rather not discuss. Can you help me with this?"

"More than anyone, yes. And if you'd like, I can speed up to your level, or we can slow it down to just-under-world-record pace. I promise you I'll not waste a second of your time, but a little bit of breathing room never hurt."

Paula let down her guard and smiled. "I'm sorry, David. I hardly mean to be a bulldozing shrew. But I am rather worried about the potential loss of income, and I suppose the fast façade is a bit of a defense."

"Perfectly understandable, Paula. Now, let's get into the thick of things. You mentioned you're head of fund-raising for a nonprofit organization. Is that what you want to continue to do?"

"Yes, absolutely. I've been in the field for nearly ten years, have an excellent reputation, and love what I do. In fact, I hope that this knowledge and commitment to one field will help me find a job fast."

"Relatively speaking, it certainly will. Many people walk through that door with only the vaguest sense of what they want to do, so your case is straightforward, and since the shortest distance between two points is always a straight line, I feel confident that we can get you a job with the greatest of ease.

Just one thing, Paula: Promise me that, in your haste—dictated by financial necessity, I understand—you won't be barrelling ahead so fast that you'll be blind to other possibilities that might come your way."

"Promised!" she enthused. "Do we get started now?"

"We've got over thirty minutes left; let's begin! We already know you want to stay in fund-raising. Are you committed to a nonprofit institution, or would you be willing to work in this capacity at a corporate entity? On first blush, it would seem that your arts programming background at prestigious foundations, coupled with your personal sophistication, would make you a leading candidate at Philip Morris, IBM, or other blue-chip companies that steward in-house foundation programs."

"I've always kept that in the back of my mind, but was afraid of getting sidetracked."

"As a goal-directed person, I know what you mean. But, Paula, let's not consider it getting sidetracked, but expanding your professional range. Okay?"

"Fine. I'm open to anything, as long as we keep our primary focus in the nonprofit area."

"Good. Next question. Are you committed to New York?"

"If I had my druthers, yes. But I'm open to relocation because I rent and, as I said, my children are at boarding school. As you probably know, Washington is a very big market for the kind of work I do, and I'm not at all averse to moving there."

"It's my hometown, and despite massive problems, can still be a very nice place to live. What about other places?"

"Anywhere and everywhere, if the job and money are right. Besides, these kinds of organizations are almost always headquartered in cities, and I can live in any one. Having said that, can we still keep New York and Washington top of mind?"

"Of course. We'll still explore all our options while placing special focus on those markets. And while you were talking, Paula, I had another thought. 'Social responsibility' seems to be a major theme in the corporate world these days, especially among young, 'hip,' growing firms. I'm thinking out loud here: Nike, Microsoft, Benetton. Would you be opposed to writing to these firms and positioning yourself as an expert in creating arts programs for the public good?"

"Not at all. Is that what you mean by pitching?"

"That's exactly what I mean. Now I see we have about ten minutes left in our session, so let's make a fast target employer plan. The first is easy. You're a fund-raiser with a highly esteemed organization in the nonprofit world. Do you know where to find a directory of nonprofits in the United States?"

"Yes, the *Foundation Directory* is the best place to start. And I understand that this will be an important element of my campaign . . . but what I'd like to do is just sit down and list all the organizations at which I know the president or executive director, because I think my personal influence will put me in good stead there."

"Brilliant; that's what we call networking. So for next week, come up with that list and a compilation of the American foundations and not-for-profit institutions for which you'd most like to work—say two hundred or so."

"What about the private companies?"

"We'll do that next week. If you were unemployed, I'd have you do that too, but since you still have a job, I'd rather you spent your time polishing and perfecting this key hit list."

"Wonderful. Just one last question, David; what should I write these names and numbers on—file cards, log them in my computer, or write them on a yellow legal pad?"

"Paula, my dear, that's entirely up to you. Use whichever system works best for you. Just remember to bring a hard copy of the names next week, whether they be handwritten or printed out from your computer."

"Will do. I look forward to seeing you then."

• • •

The next week, Paula returned just as I thought she would—utterly and totally prepared, with some extra credit work to boot.

Her first completed assignment was indeed a masterwork. "I know that we're going to do some mass targeted mailings, but I couldn't help but think that people who know my reputation would be exponentially more likely to lend an ear—and maybe even give me a job." Paula was right on both counts: Networking with those who know and respect your work is always the first order of business, whether you're looking for a freelance or full-time job.

With this letter, in one fell swoop, she had found her perfect networking pitch:

Mr. Pierre Lachaise
Executive Director
Institut des Arts Français Contemporains
555 Fifth Avenue
New York, NY 11111

Dear Pierre:

So lovely to see you at Gigi Petropinto's fête for the new artists' cooperative. (Psychedelically painted body parts are hardly my thing, but the young'uns—bless their hearts—seemed to be having a field day.)

One tries, Pierre, to wear the proverbial stiff upper lip; but by now, *mon cher,* you know the news: My foundation is consolidating with our Philadelphia branch, and blood will be spilled. (I'm sure there's performance art to be gleaned from that, but I'm too spent to think about it just now.) I haven't any idea whether mine will be among it, but I'm not playing the martyr just to find out.

To that end, I was wondering if we might have lunch next week. (I know you adore Fruits des Mers on Madison— my treat!) You always have your finger on the pulse of just what's going on in the nonprofit and arts communities, and I'd love to ask your advice on my next move.

I'll call Sophie-Hélène soon to set up a luncheon meeting with you. In the meantime, dear Pierre, my very best.

En avant!

Paula Barnes

I shouldn't have been surprised that Paula's note was letter-perfect; after all, elegant schmoozing is the key ingredient of every fund-raiser's job. Let's examine, note by note, why this letter is so damn good.

1. It virtually sings "Paula Barnes"—and your letter should call out your name just as loud, upbeat, and clear. It's always important to let your personality shine through in pitches both written and verbal, and when it comes to pitching to people you know, this is especially true.

2. Seldom is heard a discouraging word, as the patriotic ole tune goes! Oh, sure, you can refer to impending Black Fridays with a healthy dose of sarcasm, but don't let gloom and doom take over as the letter's (or phone call's) predominant theme. Paula sounds like a real trouper, ready to take on the world—in marked contrast to some soon-to-be-fired or -downsized employees who cower in corners like mice.

   Note Paula's amusing use of the French *"En avant!"* —"forward," to you and me—which puts the finishing touch on her optimistic outlook. Don't, however, go overboard with foreign words and phrases unless you're really fluent in the language. At best, this is a tactic that can underscore your camaraderie with the addressee; at worst, you'll look like a fool. (I grimace every time I hear southern Californians try to speak grotesque high school Spanish with fifth-generation, university-educated Mexican Americans as if the color of their skin alone precluded English as a mother tongue. On the other hand, if you do speak good, grammatically correct Spanish—or German or Swahili or French—native speakers will be charmed, especially if your accent is sweet.)

3. Paula is asking Pierre out to lunch. Boys and girls, I don't care how rich someone is, a free lunch is always a treat. (And for those of us who aren't, an invitation is cause for celebration!) By the way, my experience has shown that, when it's obvious you're about to lose your job, 90 percent of the human race will end up taking *you* out to lunch, even if you invited *them*. (When the invitee has a known expense account, you can pretty much bank on this being the case.)

4. Most important of all: Nowhere in this letter is Paula actually asking for a job. In effect, she doesn't have to: Pierre and anyone else with an IQ of 100—no, 90!—will "get" that she's looking for a job, and of course will apprise her of one in their organization that might be right for her. The luncheon—or meeting, if you're not the lunching type—thus beckons as a less-than-odious experience, and will allow Paula to put her feelers out, while reminding Pierre in gentle fashion of her talents and skills.

Is it more work to tailor your letter to each person on your list? Of course it is; as I intone repeatedly throughout this book, *pitching is work!* It is, however, work that pays off—and nowhere is this more apparent than when you pitch to people you know.

Paula then presented me with her mass pitch letter, which she planned on sending to about 250 nonprofit organizations and foundations on the East Coast. (As I suspected, her first-round list of targets was as pretty as a picture.)

Ms. Francine Foundation
765 Avenue of the Arts
Boston, MA 00000

Dear Ms. Foundation:

I am currently writing to determine your need of a fund-raising professional in the not-for-profit world.

Although I am currently head of this department for the Foundation for the Arts, it appears that a rash downsizing of our organization is imminent. Thus, I am presently exploring opportunities with other foundations, arts councils, and the like.

A graduate of Wellesley, I have spent the last ten years in successively responsible programming and fund-raising posts at arts organizations of the first rank. Most notable is my recent Big Arts Bang Y'all! (BABY) program that raised $10 million for young artists in the rural American South.

A résumé is enclosed for your review. Should my background be of interest to you, I would be happy to meet with you. Thank you.

Sincerely,

Paula Barnes

In a flash, Paula has gone from brilliant to banal. What's wrong with her letter?

1. Pitching is about seduction, not hitting the pitchee over the head. Never ask for a job right off the bat. Rather—and this holds whatever your job might be—paint yourself as the most attractive candidate your target employer has ever seen, one they'd be crazy to be without.

2. The only bad news any pitch letter should contain is when it precedes a clause that serves to counter an objection (i.e.: "The bad news is that my beloved organization will soon be melding into our Philadelphia branch. The good news is that I'm now free to explore new vistas in the nonprofit world"). Also, never denigrate your present employer (which Paula does subtly by using the judgmental phrase, "rash downsizing"), even though you think smashing your boss's head in with a hammer would be too kind a fate. (The dental scene in the movie

Marathon Man is my personal fantasy of fascist vengeance for people who done me wrong!)

3. To the best of your ability—whether in writing, or, as we'll see in the interview section, in person—seal the deal. Thus, instead of the passive, "Should my background be of interest to you, please call me," write:

   (a) "I'll call soon to set up a meeting convenient to your schedule" when the company or organization is on your primary hit list.

   (b) "I would relish the opportunity to describe my achievements in our field further with you. Please call me at (213) 666-6666 if you think a meeting makes sense" is the closing to use when you don't plan to follow up with a call. (It's a purely personal thing—actually a proven tactic in direct mail marketing—but I always like to restate my phone number as a call to action, even though it's obviously part of one's letterhead.)

As an immediate antidote, we drafted the following pitch letter, which, given Paula's excellent preparation of target names and addresses, she could begin using immediately:

Mr. Peter Profitless
President
American Organization for the Arts
2525 "N" Street, NW
Washington, DC 20000

Dear Mr. Profitless:

Can one woman raise $10 million for a new arts program in just six months?

If the woman is me, and the program is my hugely successful BABY, the answer is yes. Serving as chief fundraiser for this venture, which garnered international media attention, was a labor of love and perhaps the crowning glory of my ten-year arts foundation career.

Among my other achievements:

- Spearheaded the Women in Arts program that resulted in a $7.5 million grant budget and provided magnificent opportunities for unheralded new artists.

- Created and implemented a "profit partners" program, in which our organization brought in corporate arts sponsors for long-term programs—and, over five years, nearly $15 million in funding for arts activities nationwide.

- As programming director (1985 to 1989) at this organization, presided over all areas of creative and program development for this major arts institution.

Might you have need of a seasoned fund-raising and programming veteran who can work wonders even in these underfunded times? If so, please call me at (212) 111-1111; I'd love to meet.

Best and thanks,

Paula Barnes

This time around, Paula is presented as a winner—not merely a seat-warmer, but a proactive, results–oriented professional whose personal trademarks are a love for her field and the desire to accomplish only great things. She has found her Perfect Pitch, and you can bet that any foundation that is even thinking about adding staff—and maybe, by dint of her don't-pass-this-one-by pitch, even some that aren't—will see her posthaste.

Here, note that Paula could have elected to close with, "I will be in Washington soon to explore opportunities there, and will call to arrange a meeting convenient to you."

Note also that sending a résumé is optional in this case. As a marketeer, I firmly believe in teasing the target; the object here is to make them virtually beg for more. (I've actually sold books on short, Perfect Pitches as opposed to the more standard long prospecti.) If Paula were switching industries, she definitely would not want to include a résumé, which would confuse the issue and serve only to confound a wonderful cover letter pitch. But in this case, because it's like-like, including a résumé is up to her. My experience shows that the general rules here are as follows:

1. If you've got a steady, uninterrupted flow of work experience and a strong educational background, send the résumé.

2. If there's something you're trying to hide, or you've worked in several different industries, don't send it. Anything that serves to distract from your Perfect Pitch— lack of a degree, years of unemployment, jail time— should be swept under the carpet until it absolutely has to rear its ugly head. By then, you'll have so endeared yourself to your target that the impact will, de facto, be assuaged. Why close a door before it's even opened?

As I mentioned, Paula had already done her extra-credit work, a letter to private industry. Surprisingly, this pitch was the polar opposite of her less-than-impactful letter within her own field. Innately, she knew that to convince companies that they needed an arts program, she had to pitch and pitch hard; this is what she wrote:

> Mr. Yasuhisa Yamato
> President and CEO
> GINJA ELECTRONICS
> 33 Perfect Way
> Cupertino, CA 99999
>
> Dear Mr. Yamato:
>
> Have you ever wondered how your competitors gained such wonderful visibility by sponsoring charitable foundations, arts programs, and the like?
>
> They start by using people like me, whose extensive involvement in the nonprofit arts community allows them to create programs that garner international media attention and create positive consumer impressions of your company like nothing else can.
>
> As a fund-raising and programming professional with one of America's most prestigious and visible arts organizations, I am among the country's recognized authorities in my field. (Press stories and a professional biography, enclosed, will tell you more.)
>
> Many companies earmark funds for charitable purposes in all areas without really knowing if they're getting the best bang for the buck. This is my special expertise; and if you've been considering making changes in your "for the public good" programs—or starting one up—shouldn't we talk?

Please phone me at (212) 111-1111 if this is a subject you'd like to explore.

Cordially,

Paula Barnes

You'll notice immediately that Paula isn't importuning a job; rather, she's positioning herself as an eminent authority in her field. Why hasn't she included the phrase, "I'll call you soon" in this pitch? Because she has stated her premise clearly and winningly; if there's any interest at all on the part of the chief executive to whom she has written, she will be contacted. Also, because it's more than likely that person will pass Paula's letter on to the company's publicity head or outside agency, she may well be barking up the wrong tree. The trick for Paula (or anyone else, in any field) is to present herself—by dint of a recitation of her achievements, enclosure of press citations, awards, etc.—as such a mover and shaker that a hiring authority will want to know who she is, regardless of whether a job opening exists. Keep this operating premise close to your heart, and your pitch will be perfect every time!

7

Sleuthing: Uncovering Hidden Jobs Even Before They Occur

"Whew!" you say. "I've spent endless hours playing my contacts, writing to headhunters, pitching to people I'd like to work for, and answering ads. I'm bushed! But at least my job is done, right?"

Sorry, Charlie (or Charlene). You done good, but you ain't done it all. So listen up, and listen well: The scoop I'm about to share with you may well be the one that gets you your next consulting assignment, freelance work, or full-time job.

In the best of all possible worlds, you'd be so hooked in to the executive turntable that you could sense staffing changes even before they occurred. But the world ain't perfect (touché, Monsieur Voltaire), and even though you've networked your little fanny to death, there's no way you—or anyone—could know everything that's going on in even a highly defined segment of the corporate world.

Luckily—*very* luckily for you!—there's a wonderful way to know who's doing what, where. They're obscure items of information called newspapers and trade magazines, and if you don't already, you should be reading at least several a week from cover to back.

When I was hired as head of video marketing for New Line Cinema, the country's largest independent film studio, major articles appeared in the entertainment trade dailies as well as the "Executive Suite" column in the *Los Angeles Times*. I was pleased to see these announcements. Not to glorify my own achievements (though like everyone else, I secretly hoped the jocks who tortured me in high school—hopefully serving life sentences in a Turkish prison—would see them), but so potential job applicants would start writing to me in droves. I needed to staff up soon, and felt certain that eager beavers would be beating a path to my door. (After all, sighting a notice of my boss's appointment and my subsequent pitch letter was what got me my job!)

Guess how many letters actually arrived. 500? (That's half of the typical responses for a glam job in the *Los Angeles Times*.) 250? 100? 10? Nope. Guess again, folks.

The answer is (drum roll, please): 0. Zip. Nothing. *Nada*. Oh, several of my old vendors (graphic designers, copywriters, and such) picked up the phone to congratulate me (and to look for work), but this was a relative no-brainer requiring no special pitch. But not a single new person wrote or called.

If I ever felt that I was living in a parallel universe, the time was then. Was I crazy, or what? Here we were, in the middle of one of California's worst recessions, with hundreds and hundreds of midlevel entertainment executives out of work. How could it be that not one of them was reading the *Hollywood Reporter, Variety,* and the *L.A. Times*?

I'll tell you this, my friends: When I was out of work, I woke up at dawn to be the first one on the block (nay, in the city!) to see what was going on in the corporate world. And that meant perusing the executive shuffle columns in the above-mentioned publications, plus *L.A. Business Journal,* the *Wall Street Journal,* the *New York Times;* and, on a weekly basis, *Billboard, Video Weekly, Video Insider, Video Store, Adweek, Brandweek, Mediaweek,* and *Advertising Age.* (Among them, I felt I had the no-stone-unturned category pretty well covered—and I did.)

But apparently, not one single human being in southern California or beyond thought to do the same. You'll excuse my hyperbolic exasperation, but I view the situation with the same amazement today that I did three years ago. Any good candidate at the marketing coordinator, manager, or director level in video or a related industry (TV, records, theatrical films) would have been called in to interview in three seconds flat, and, moreover, would have had a damn good shot at one of several available jobs. Instead, it took the "bending over backwards" move of a display ad in the Hollywood trades to evoke a response—and even then, I got only the lackluster, virtually "pitchless" response I mentioned in the beginning of this book.

I think you get the point. Whether you be searching for a full-time job, consulting gig, or freelance work, you must devote time each week to reading publications that tell you what's going on—and, equally as important—who's going where in the business world. I'm not a schoolmarm, thus I'll not presume to tell you how many hours you need to devote to this task. Personally, I think you should read business page features and trade magazine articles with an eagle eye to know what's really happening in that part (your part!) of the world, but whether you choose to do so or just scan executive roster news is up to you.

By the way, this activity is not just the domain of the executive set. Just refer to the brilliant job hunt conducted by a su-persecretary, Eliza (one of my favorite stories ever!), later in this chapter, and you'll see how important a bird's-eye view of the corporate shuffle can be to your own campaign.

Beginning now, keep a running list of all the publications you need to read or scan as an integral part of your search. Don't just think of them; *write them down.* I don't care if you use file cards, a computer, or toilet paper, but put this list in writing. Write each publication's name in your diary on the day of the week when it comes out, use easily movable Post-its, or devise your own system; you're big boys and girls. If you can afford subscriptions, this becomes a no-brainer, but if you, like me, would rather go to the library or buy newsstand copies, you need to know exactly when the pub date for each paper and magazine is. The point (have I driven it home hard enough?) is *not to miss a single source, ever.* On those rare occasions when I myself have, and hear of a great lead via a friend, I feel like a real jerk. (If you're less hard on yourself, feel free to feel like a semi-jerk.)

As a general guide, if you are conducting a job search, you should be regularly reading:

- Your city's major metropolitan daily newspaper, with special emphasis on the business section
- Your industry's trade newspapers, magazines, and newsletters

If you are looking for a position in the business world, this must be augmented by thorough and constant perusal of the following:

- *New York Times*
- *Wall Street Journal*
- Your city or region's business trade paper (examples include *L.A. Business Journal, South Florida Business Week, Crain's New York Business,* etc.). The business reference librarian in the biggest city near you can tell you which publication(s) serve(s) your area; or visit a newsstand and conduct your own search.

In today's "Executive Suite" column of the *Los Angeles Times,* for example, these are just some of the new hires and promotions that were announced.

- Senior VP, Publicity, at New Line Cinema
  (Calling on-staff publicists, freelance publicists, freelance writers, catering companies, premium manufacturers, designers, limousine company owners, floral shop owners, and secretaries—and that's just for starters!)
- Senior VP, Production, at Walt Disney Pictures
  (Calling all writers—who in L.A. *doesn't* have a screenplay?—script readers, production managers, set designers, development staffers, executive secretaries, etc.)
- Senior VP, International Marketing, at Columbia TriStar
  (Calling all entertainment marketing executives, publicists, promotions managers—and, of course, anyone fluent in foreign languages will have a real leg up here.)
- Chief operating officer at Hallmark Entertainment
  (Jackpot! This guy's the head honcho, the kingpin, the emperor of the kingdom. Anyone involved in any aspect

of the entertainment industry who's looking for a job, consultancy, or freelance work should be writing to this guy—production executives, marketeers, salespeople, international types, secretaries, lawyers, accountants, advertising, and public relations agencies, designers, agents. A notice like this is a virtual gold mine in this one-industry town!)

- VP of the Black Music Division at MCA Records
  (A little research is needed here. Is the newly named exec only in charge of A&R—that would be my guess—or is it a self-contained division in which this person oversees all advertising, publicity, and promotions as well as artist development? A quick phone call to his assistant or MCA's publicity department and a little ingenuity will get you the answer. I'd say, "Hi, this is David from Black Entertainment Television, and I was happy to read of Mr. So-and-so's appointment to MCA in the paper today." (Butter them up first by asking, "What artists are on your label?") Then: "Great! And will Mr. So-and-so be in charge of promotional activities as well as A&R?" By rights, such information shouldn't be given out to just anyone, but unfortunately a sense of confidentiality and propriety is an antiquated concept in most companies today, and a little probing can elicit much more information than it really should. (Even without making a call, certain job hunters should send off a pitch note posthaste: A&R people, recording facilities, service companies—the above mentioned limos, flowers, and food, to name an obvious few—secretaries, publicity folks, etc.)

- Senior VP, General Counsel, at Paramount Pictures (This is a veritable beacon for all attorneys, paralegals, contract administrators, legal secretaries, and outside law firms, who are almost always used to supplement in-house efforts.)

If, fortuitously, you should see the name of a friend, colleague, or former boss (one who likes you, natch), you're in great luck: Pick up the phone and congratulate him or her that very day. Chances are that person is still reveling in the glow of their newfound success and will treat you with the kindness of Little Miss Sunshine, even if they're normally the types who'd push their mothers off a train to get ahead; why not bask in their glow (however temporary it may be)? And since you weren't born yesterday, I don't have to tell you that if you are a

Job seeker: Hit them up with the time-honored question, "Will you be adding people to your staff?"; then, whatever their response, draft a letter to them posthaste; or

Freelancer or consultant: Congratulate them again, then ask for a meeting later that week. (If they're "too busy," "need time to get adjusted," or "need to review their boss's needs," etc., write a fabulous pitch note, send it off, then call them next week.)

If you don't personally know the lucky ones, you should send off a classic pitch letter anyway (this, of course, will constitute the lion's share of cases). But first, here's an example of the kind of letter 95 percent of people write:

SAMSON STONE
123 Bible Way
Ancient, CA 99999

Mr. Roberto Dinero
Senior Vice President, Marketing
DOLL BABY, INC.
444 Executive Path
Bigwig, CA 99999

Dear Mr. Dinero:

I was interested to read of your promotion in *Toy & Hobby World* Magazine.

In the hope that you might be hiring new staff, I am enclosing my résumé for your review. I am currently a product manager at Comtoy Inc., but feel that my career path is limited here, and am therefore seeking new opportunities.

I am experienced in all areas of toy marketing, including advertising, product management, and sales promotion. I would be happy to meet with you to discuss my background further.

Thank you.

Sincerely,

Samson Stone

Do I really need to tell you what's wrong with this letter? By this stage of the game, I think you've probably already figured it out, but just to hammer the point home, here goes:

Two egregious errors jump out:

1. Almost every sentence begins with the word *I*. Not only is this unimaginative syntactically, it represents the kind of narcissistic point of view I discourage in the introduction of the book. To pitch, you need to tell a potential boss or hiring agent what you can do for them, something Sammy conveniently forgot to do.

2. *Never* allude to potential problems, glass ceilings, or dissatisfaction of any kind in your present job. You can bring this up (if pertinent) during an actual interview, but why slam the door with negativity before you even get your foot in the door? Leave the apologia at home.

There's nothing truly horrid about this letter; in fatter times, when competition wasn't so keen, people actually got hired by presenting themselves this way. In today's times, however, such an uninspiring pitch won't merit a second look (unless your father is a friend of the boss). The general tone of the letter is boring, bland, and flaccid; as such, it's easy to overlook.

On the other hand, let's look at a vibrant, well-planned pitch. One like this:

SUSANNAH SHORE
345 Laguna Road
Laguna Beach, CA 99999

May 9, 1997

Mr. Roberto Dinero
Senior Vice President, Marketing
DOLL BABY, INC.

444 Executive Path
Bigwig, CA 99999

Dear Mr. Dinero:

Congratulations on your sensational new post! A senior vice presidency is always a coup, and even more so with a company as prestigious as Doll Baby, Inc.

Since a thorough review of the ranks is always a first order of business, I'm sure you'll be determining your staffing needs in the weeks to come. Should you decide that a seasoned toy marketeer with a Northwestern MBA could help take your division to new heights, perhaps you'll think of me.

Among the highlights of my background:

- Six years' progressively responsible experience in the toy field
- Executive posts with Mattel, Hasbro, and Sanrio
- Product development, strategic marketing, and creative expertise

I'll call soon to see if a meeting is in order at this time. Till then, congratulations again on your wonderful new position.

Sincerely,

Susannah Shore

Note that, unlike in wide-range direct mail campaigns, Susannah chose to highlight her achievements in general terms. To someone like Roberto Dinero, who most likely will have definite jobs to fill, Susannah doesn't have to blow her trumpet all that loud; it's enough that she's a seasoned toy marketing pro. Wisely, she keeps the emphasis on Roberto's fabulous new job, rather than diverting all attention to herself. That's because, since her background and education are first-rate, Susannah will certainly be among the first called in if a position needs to be filled.

Important Note: When sending out this or any other kind of pitch letter directly to a prospective employer, write "Private" on the envelope—preferably in blue or red, so it stands out from the black type of the address. Underline or circle the word "Private" for greater effect (do not, however, adorn the letter "i" with a heart, peace sign, circle, or rub-off tattoo). You'd think everyone would do this to get past the addressee's assistant, but they don't; and when they do, people often use the clichéd "Confidential" (or, worse yet, the comical "Classified"). A few bosses have such close and trusted relationships with their assistants that they instruct them to open all mail, even that marked "Private," but trust me, they're very few. (I myself live in constant fear that my clubbing days in 1980s New York will come back to haunt me, and don't want *anyone* opening my mail!) The bottom line: Marking an envelope "Private" really works.

Very Important Note: You may have noticed that, in her letter, Susannah doesn't make the obligatory allusion to the "enclosed résumé." That's because there is none! The letter itself tells the reader all he needs to know (for now): that she is an experienced toy marketer, has a top MBA, and keeps up with changes in her industry. (Even more, the mere fact that she's writing to Roberto signals to him that Susannah is shrewd and "in touch" enough to know about his new post. In short, it flags her as a "player" in the toy game—if you'll pardon the pun!)

What a pitch like this does is to whet the appetite with tidbits too appealing to ignore. When writing, always keep this attitude in mind: If I were in the seat of the person to whom I'm pitching, what could I say that would not only stimulate my curiosity, but virtually dare them not to see me? How can I pitch myself as such a hot property that, whether or not an opening currently exists, this person will want to call me in to know who I am—and what I can do for him or her?

If you're called by the person you pitched (or, more usually, by a staff member) and asked to send a résumé, remember this cardinal rule: Be courteous (and never truculent), but always try to do so in person—that is, to wangle a meeting out of the deal. A typical conversation might go like this:

"Susannah? This is Brett in Roberto Dinero's office. Roberto has received your letter, and was wondering whether you could send him a résumé."

"I certainly can, Brett. But what I'd like to do is to present it to him in person so that we can go over my background in detail."

"Well, you know, Roberto has just started with the firm, and he's very busy. Could you just send in the résumé for now?"

"I'll tell you what, Brett. Would you please ask him whether we might arrange a meeting? I'll hold the line if you like—and just fifteen minutes of his time would be great. Is he there now?"

Harken back to the Seven Steps to a Perfect Pitch, and you'll see that what Susannah's trying to do is to seal the deal—to stay in the driver's seat, if you like. There are two possible outcomes, of course. One is that Brett is a nice person (and/or in a good mood), and so is Roberto, and a meeting is arranged.

The other is that Brett comes back to the phone and tells Susannah, "I'm sorry, but he just doesn't have time now. He asked again if you could just send the résumé for now."

"With pleasure. I'd be happy to; expect it this week. And thanks, Brett, for your call."

"You're welcome. Good-bye, Susannah."

"Good-bye, Brett. I hope to meet you soon."

Please don't fail to note that Susannah treats Brett with courtesy, friendliness, and respect. Her closing indicates to him that he's not "just an assistant" but a person in his own right, and she hopes to meet him. If said without irony or obsequiousness, people are always flattered—I know I am—that someone wants to talk to them. (It's the human condition, after all.) And I can tell you from personal experience that assistants and secretaries do influence their boss's decision to see someone or not. Michele B., my assistant at New Line, whose story I tell in the opening pages, let her opinions be known in no uncertain terms, and I'll remember her pronouncements always: from "She sounds sweet!" to "Girlfriend has an attitude problem" to a vociferous, hands-down, "Not!" In fact, Michele and I got to know each other so well that, after a candidate interviewed, no words needed be spoken: A shift of her eyes or raised eyebrows—plus rather more colorful gestures when the interviewee was Michele's physical cup of tea—were all that needed be "said."

Now, back to Susannah, whose work doesn't end there. Before sending off her letter to Roberto Dinero, she remembers to add his name, title, and address to her Rolodex and/or computer file. She also makes a note in her agenda to write to Roberto again in two months if she doesn't have a job by that time. Then, she'll write a classic pitch letter outlining her background and achievements in greater detail, while highlighting the divisional changes she knows Roberto and his team to have made through her careful perusal of toy industry trades. A letter just like this:

Dear Mr. Dinero:

As you'll certainly recall, I wrote to you shortly after your appointment as SVP at Doll Baby—and through the trades and my industry colleagues, have seen the changes you've made in just a short time.

Changes like the new Wet-A-Wee Doll and its sensational new advertising campaign . . . and the in-store events promoting Kinky Ken, the doll the whole family loves to hate!

Maybe I'm quick to recognize your efforts because innovative new products, disruptive advertising campaigns, and media-ready publicity events are my stock-in-trade. While marketing director at Mattel, I achieved results in all these areas, as follows:

PRODUCT DEVELOPMENT: Managed launch of three new Barbie line extensions, resulting in $100 million in incremental sales.

ADVERTISING: Directed creative and media aspects of $20 million ad campaign to promote this launch.

PUBLIC RELATIONS AND PROMOTIONS: Supervised public relations agency's activities on all doll lines, including a live publicity stunt that generated national coverage in the print and broadcast press.

I would love to get together to discuss my background vis-à-vis your staffing needs, and will call soon to set up an appointment convenient for you. In the meantime, thanks for your kind review.

Sincerely,

Susannah Shore

As it happens, Roberto Dinero wasn't in the position to add staff when Susannah first wrote. But two months later, he was, and Susannah's letter (which indicated her achievements in the industry, plus her recognition of Roberto's own achievements) got her right in the door—and into her own office shortly thereafter. See what a difference a Perfect Pitch can make?

Before we leave this subject, I should repeat something for clarity's sake. While you will be on the lookout for news items on executive placements in your and related industries, you should also peruse actual feature articles in newspapers and trade magazines. They almost always feature prominent people in a given industry, and are wonderful places to find out even more about key executives and their activities.

Responding in specific detail should be an integral part of your job campaign because:

1. An intelligent letter underscoring your intense knowledge of an industry, company, and the person in question reflects an inquiring, alert mind and practically demands a response—usually a kind one.

2. Very few people do this (even my clients!) because "it's just too much trouble." Here, I quote my mother, one

of whose many wise sayings is, "You get out of life what you put into it."

Of all the available tactics in your job hunt, this one may be among the most effective. I know this because I've gotten many an interview—and, subsequently, was referred to myriad colleagues of people I'd interviewed with—on the merit of my go-get-'em attitude.

And I've been on the other side of the desk, too. While at Media Home Entertainment, the largest independent home video company in the nation (until it was swallowed whole by Fox Video), I talked my way into an interview in *Video Insider* magazine on the fascinating, earth-shaking subject of in-store POPs. (That's point-of-purchase displays, to those of you in nonmerchandising fields.) Shortly after the article appeared, I got a wonderful note from a young woman I'll call Jane Aire:

> Dear David:
>
> Though we haven't spoken since last year's VSDA, I wanted to let you know how insightful I thought your comments on POP distribution and design were.
>
> As manager of sales promotion at Home Alone Video, I share many of your concerns, and feel they've been long overlooked by the industry. In fact, I look forward to implementing exciting new programs as soon as possible.
>
> What I'd like more than anything is to apply my knowledge of merchandising and promotion at Media Home Entertainment. A five-year veteran of the video field, I actually got my start behind a counter while still in college. (Do you need further proof I'm a video freak?)

To further acquaint you with my background, a résumé is enclosed. I'll call soon to discuss getting together with you.

Till then, my best,

Jane Aire

First, a footnote: I don't think I ever actually met Jane, at VSDA (the national video convention) or anywhere else. (I have the uncanny knack of remembering names and faces from grade school—how weird is that?) But most people forget people they met five minutes ago, and would easily be fooled by Jane's presumption; some would even feel a twinge of guilt at not remembering her. But her note was so on target that I couldn't refuse meeting her. (Note: Jane's letter was good, but not great; if I had written it, I would have gone into a specific point or two about POPs, illustrating an analytical, not just reflective, point of view.)

As it happened, there was no place for Jane on my team. She was a sweet person and reasonably smart, but not really a hard-hitter; I was looking for a seasoned marketeer, preferably with experience in the packaged goods field. But in several months' time, remembering her good qualities, I referred her to a colleague at a medium-sized video firm—one who would have been bowled over by a Stanford MBA but who liked an above-average team player like Jane just fine. She got a job with a better title and 20 percent pay raise at his firm, and was by all accounts very happy there—all because of the initiative she took in writing to me. And you can achieve just as wonderful results by keeping an eye on the business press.

As I said earlier, pitching in response to staffing changes reported in the trade and consumer press is a tactic everyone can use. Just consider the case of Eliza, one of my favorite clients of all time.

When I met Eliza Zane, I was immediately impressed by her self-confidence and poise. There's a thin line between arrogance and self-possession, and Eliza knew just where to tread: She was strong without being overbearing, and exerted her personal attractiveness without being flirty. In the most obvious terms, she was pitching herself as a winner, and that's exactly how she was perceived by me.

(This quality, alas, is something no book can teach; I laugh when reading the ones that try. We have our strong points, and that elusive trait known as poise is among the most difficult to achieve. Some people are born with it, and they're the lucky ones—in some ways, their pitch is themselves, and we've all seen cases where it's not the best or brightest, but those who position themselves as such, who make it to the top. Others of us have to work at it, and I'm still trying to get it right.)

Eliza was a sharp, supereffective secretary in a small, unsexy firm that offered nowhere for her to go. And for someone of her skills and drive, stalling midstream was definitely not in Eliza's long-range plans.

Like all Perfect Pitchers, Eliza took stock of her strengths, her goals, and—very importantly—employment trends in her field. What she saw: companies dropping secretaries like flies in favor of voice mail and fancy computer systems. What she read (clever Eliza made sure to scan the business section of the paper every day): The number of jobs for lower-level secretaries was decreasing nationwide; well-trained executive assistants, however, were in great demand. (Eliza recalled a recent article in the *Los Angeles Times* in which top execs bemoaned the dearth of secretaries with top English, computer, and interpersonal skills.)

So what am I—chopped liver? Eliza mused. Not for nothing did I take every computer course that came my way . . . and haven't all my bosses complimented me on my great writing skills?

In short order, Eliza decided to wage an all-out war to get herself hired as a high-level executive aide. Like most of us, she first made the rounds of employment agencies, where she was treated like yesterday's news. (As we'll see clearly in Chapter 13, "Pitching to Change Careers," neither a headhunter nor a personnel agency will go out of their way to help you forge new professional paths; you've got to do this yourself.)

"Honey," one wizened job counselor told her, "I got executive assistants with ten years' experience looking for jobs. You're a nice girl, but you're just a secretary. Be happy with what you got."

Just a secretary? Eliza silently stewed. Not on your life—*honey!* For Eliza, as for most people who eventually achieve success, this rude turndown provided the greatest incentive of all to show the naysayers wrong.

So Eliza got crackin'; with the firmest resolve, she mounted her attack. But before she could pitch, she needed to know *whom* to pitch. Living in a "one-industry town" like L.A., that wasn't hard to figure out. (Do you live in Akron? Houston? Montreal? You already know what your city's biggest industries are, and by keeping in touch with the business news, you'll know even more.) If entertainment chieftains didn't need a capable right-hand person, who did? Great, Eliza thought. But where do I find out who and where they are?

A trip to her local library solved that problem fast. The reference librarian (a profession whose virtues all pitchers extol!) pointed Eliza to an annual executive roster of film, TV, and recording companies published by a major trade magazine. "What a godsend!" Eliza enthused. "Every name in town is here."

"So now what?" she asked herself. "How do I make these people want to know me?"

After chewing the end of her pen for an hour or two, Eliza had a classic "Eureka!" moment. But of course, she thought. I have to tell these people what I can do for them. So she listed her strengths in whatever order they came to her, as follows:

- Some college
- Five years' experience
- Fast typing and shorthand
- Literate in five computer languages
- Fast learner
- Great organizer
- Takes care of things before they're asked for
- Works long hours without balking
- Cool clothes (Well, why not—I'm far too trendy to keep working in this dump!)

Then Eliza considered an even more important question: Which of these qualities would be of most interest to somebody who might hire me? And what proposition could I make that would be strong enough to get their attention—and maybe want them to meet with me first?

All good secretaries have fine office skills; that was a given. What Eliza thought set her ahead of the pack were her talents for organizing, working fast (wasn't she always the first one to finish projects and ask for more?), and solving problems of all sizes for her boss.

So, pen in hand, she drafted the following pitch:

Dear Ms. Super-Exec:

An executive secretary who can read your mind: fact or fiction?

In my case, the former is definitely true. During my five-year secretarial career, I have put out fires, Xeroxed mountains, and charmed my way into flight upgrades galore for my boss.

I can also:

- Use every computer program known to man (well, almost every one—and even spread sheets don't freak me out!)
- Turn the most antiquated filing systems into information superhighways
- Dazzle you with a work ethic like you wouldn't believe

In addition to top-notch skills, I am upbeat, stylish, and an eternal optimist.

If you're on the lookout for an executive assistant of the first rank, shouldn't we meet? I look forward to doing so soon.

Sincerely,

Eliza Z.

P.S.: If you're fully staffed but know a colleague who may be looking for someone like me, won't you pass my résumé on? Kind thanks.

Now, face it: How many letters like Eliza's have you seen? Most pitches—for jobs, services, whatever—are as dry as dirt. But the one Eliza penned grabbed the reader from the very first line.

Granted, her letter—kissed with wit and a touch of bravado —wouldn't have worked in an ultraconservative banking firm unless the recipient were uncharacteristically loose-laced. (Had that been her goal, she could have listed her abilities in a more straightforward, less spunky way.) But if your goal is a position with a company in a creative business, a pitch infused with passion and humor can work like a charm.

It certainly did in Eliza's case: She sent out 100 letters, secured six interviews, and landed a job as a personal assistant to a senior vice president with a major TV network. (Interestingly, the job actually resulted from one of the "pass-alongs" effected by the P.S. on her letter—a technique I encourage in all but the most targeted mailings.)

8
· · ·

Pitching in Response to Job Ads or You *Will* Be Seen!

Practically everyone who's ever looked for a job has been given the following very bad advice:

Don't waste your time answering ads in the paper.
Nobody ever gets jobs that way.

An application of simple logic will negate this argument in a New York minute. Papers are chock full of classified and display ads day in and day out, and companies wouldn't waste their money to advertise if the whole thing were a silly game.

Should responding to ads be your only job-hunting strategy? Of course not. But should you ignore this tactic entirely? Not on your life!

What the naysayers might better have told you is this:

Most people answer want ads in an uninspired and ultimately inefficient manner that practically assures they won't get the job.

As someone who's received countless résumés during his fifteen-year business career, I can vouch that the above is true. As much as 90 percent of letters sound something like this:

Mr. David Andrusia
Director of Marketing
ABC Cosmetics Corporation
New York, NY 00000

Dear Mr. Andrusia:

I am writing to respond to the ad for a marketing manager in Sunday's *New York Times*.

I am presently working as a marketing manager at DEF, Inc., on the Rescue Hair Care Line (approximate annual sales $60 million). Prior to this position, I was assistant product manager at XYZ Enterprises, working in the same product category.

It would be my pleasure to meet to discuss my background in further detail. A résumé is enclosed.

Thank you.

Sincerely,

Bobbi Bland

How bad is the aptly named Ms. Bland's letter? Pretty bad, but not horrible, and here's why: She was working in the same industry (health and beauty aids) as the recipient of the letter, and might well get in the door on that strength alone. (As I said before, this certainly would have been the case at an earlier point in America's history; but given the ultracompetitive climate of today, she'd have a much tougher time with so soft a sell now.)

Worse yet, people who are not in the same industry often send just this kind of letter; doing so is nothing less than waste of good (I hope) stationery and a thirty-two-cent stamp. Would

I see people who held the position of marketing manager in a different industry? I might, but they'd have to convince me first.

It is possible—definitely possible!—even in these downsized times. But you can't just present your slightly off-target credentials and pray someone will see a fit. *You have to pitch.*

Let's say, for example, that you're a marketing manager, but not in the cosmetics industry. Then, put your shoes in the place of the hiring authority. Is there any way you can pitch your credentials credibly and warrant consideration for the job? As in Marketing 101, the first question, Should we market (this product or service)? becomes Should we pitch? There are only two possible answers: yes and no.

In other words, can you realistically market your background and skills in a compelling enough way to be of interest to the pitchee? To find the answer, I suggest doing this: In chart form, write down the industry, its distribution points, and the responsibilities of the job. For instance:

	Advertised Position	**Your Job**
Title	Marketing Manager	Marketing Manager
Industry	Cosmetics	Toys
Distribution	Class	Mass; Some Class
Years Experience	Seeks Five	Four
Job Responsibilities	Product Management	Yes
	Product Development	Some
	Advertising Management	Yes
	Publicity Management	Minimal
	Profit & Loss Management	Yes

The above chart shows that, while there isn't a perfect fit, candidates holding the position of marketing manager with a toy company had enough similar points of experience in their background to pitch themselves, but they would have to concoct an ingenious, well-constructed pitch even to merit consideration. (This is especially true at a time when many people with years of cosmetics experience are out of work.)

In this kind of trans-industry pitch, you don't have a choice: You have to come up with a preemptive pitch that translates your experience into a seemingly flawless match. After all, as any experienced pitchmeister (should I say pitchmädchen to be politically correct?) knows, you have to place yourself in the chair of the person receiving the pitch. If the target—be it a personnel manager or the hiring authority him- or herself—is also receiving scores of résumés from people already in the cosmetics field, why should he or she even consider yours?

The way to do this is to parrot back the particulars of the ad, drawing parallels to your own experience. Something like this would be near perfect:

Dear Mr. Andrusia:

As a marketeer with a special interest in fashion and five years' experience in blue-chip firms, I believe my background qualifies me for consideration of the marketing manager position advertised in the *New York Times* on May 5, 1997.

Among the highlights of my background:

PRODUCT DEVELOPMENT: At Comtoy, I ideated and launched six new products, including the Fanny Fashion Doll—

named doll introduction of the year by an industry trade magazine.

ADVERTISING: Developed advertising and promotional budgets, and supervised Creative and Media for a $20 million annual expenditure.

PUBLICITY: Worked with store management and our publicity firm to implement a series of national promotions supporting Fanny Fashion launch—generating an average store traffic increase of 60 percent.

SALES PROMOTION: Conceived and supervised production of all packaging and displays for ten major product lines.

While the toy business has proved stimulating and expanded my range of professional expertise, fashion is my passion, and it's time I made my move into the cosmetics world where I belong. The present opening appears to be one in which I can do just that, while drawing on my own experience to take your business to new heights.

It would be my pleasure to meet to discuss my background with you. In the meantime, thank you for your kind review.

Sincerely,

Bobbi Bright

Now, isn't that much better? Yes, but it's still not enough. The chance of your letter arriving on a sympathetic desk in the personnel department of a medium-to-large-sized firm is only about 25 percent. With a new and improved pitch letter like the one above, you're augmenting your chances of being seen and heard, but most midlevel personnel people are still looking for an "apple to apple" fit in response to an ad.

So here comes your Perfect Pitch. If the ad is a job you'd give your left arm for, and it's one in which you realistically think you could excel, your work's not done yet, because writing to the personnel department isn't enough: You have to pitch directly to the person who's hiring for that job.

Surprisingly, this isn't all that hard to do. Typically, an ad contains tons of clues—some obvious, others more oblique. To master the puzzle, this is what to do:

1. If the company's name is listed, for instance, Almay, your work is over: call the company and find out who the VP of Marketing is, and send your pitch to him or her.

2. Even if no company is listed, clues can abound. If the ad says "major French-based cosmetics company," you've only got a few choices: Lancôme, YSL, Dior, and Orlane come directly to mind. Call their public relations office and ask, "Who's the head of Marketing, please?" There's only one response, and whether that person holds the title of VP, senior VP, executive VP, or anything else, you'll be writing to the person in charge.

    Similarly, if you're a chemical engineer, and an ad in the *Wall Street Journal* "Employment Weekly" is advertising "blind," the giveaway words might be "Louisiana petroleum company." Ostensibly—nay, certainly!—if you're already in the field, you'll have some idea who the major players in the Louisiana oil game are. And even if you don't know them off the top of your head, you

should have—or should easily find—rosters of companies in your field. Then, a simple phone call (as in the
example above) will reveal whom to write to.

What we're talking about, then, is a two-tiered approach,
which falls easily under the leave-no-stone-unturned banner.
There's one other big plus about writing directly to the hiring
authority: You can use a far more persuasive and individualized
pitch than you can with a Personnel-directed ad.

Let's return to the example of the toy marketeer who was
dying to get into cosmetics. Bobbi (whose last name I've transformed from Bland to Bright) could write a winning pitch like
this:

Mr. David Andrusia
Marketing Director
Cosmetics ABC

Dear Mr. Andrusia:

For three years, I've made America's top-selling rag doll
line a total knockout. Now I'd like to help make real
women gorgeous, too.

As marketing manager at Terrific Toys, I wrote the marketing plan that ultimately produced Very Violet, the
best-selling fashion doll in her category. Along the way,
I managed all advertising and promotional activities, including one of the best-attended, highest-profile in-store
events in Bloomingdale's history.

But what can I say? I'm a girlie, and my real passion is
painting my face. Pop quiz? I can name every shade of

lipstick your company has put out in the past five years (and probably most of your competitors', too!).

I hold a BA and MBA from the University of Michigan, and know that my marketing expertise and ability to tell fuschia from magenta in dim light would help propel your division to beautiful new heights.

Can we meet?

Sincerely,

Bella Blue

Would Bella's letter work in a conservative industry like banking or management consulting? Not unless (and this is highly unlikely) the recipient was as spunky, sassy, and savvy as she. But in a fashion-oriented environment like cosmetics, only the hardest heart could ignore her plucky point of view.

I'd see someone like Bella with pleasure. In fact, when I was at the movie studio, I always wanted someone to write and tell me not just where they had worked and what they had done, but how seeing *The Conformist* changed their life. Nobody ever did. *People want people who are full of life, verve, and love what they do. Convince them in your pitch that this is exactly the kind of person you are!*

Note: The best-written pitches sound as if you were speaking directly to the addressee, with the intended effect that you are actually there in the room with them. With the exception of the few remaining superstuffy law firms or consulting concerns, where a by-the-book approach still applies, the goal of your letter should be to inform and to charm. The faux-Anglophilic, ridiculously stilted English found in erstwhile career guides should be considered the cultural artifact that it is. ("In the eventuality of a suitable opening in your firm, mightn't you be kind enough to advise me of any attractive situation that might occur?" is a particularly risible example of this outdated syntactical style.)

The Cardinal Rules of Answering Ads

1. If you're responding to a classified ad for a secretarial, part-time, or other nonexecutive position, call or write immediately. In most cases, people want to fill support positions immediately, and will be glad to hear from a qualified applicant like you.

2. If you're responding to an ad for a technical or managerial position (most of which are in display ads), wait five business days before responding. Most people respond at once; by waiting, you'll not only avoid getting lost in the crowd, but will stand out by virtue of the recency effect (which holds that the résumé most recently received is the one a hiring authority remembers).

3. When it's a job to die for at a company that's on your must-have list, take the time to tailor your résumé to fit the job to a T. Fifteen years ago, this was almost impossible; with today's wizardrous computers, it's a veritable breeze. For instance, if the job advertised is director of publicity and your last title was director of marketing yet you managed all public relations activities, change your title to director of advertising and publicity. Altering your job title slightly is no crime; changing the description of what you did is a pretty big lie.

- If your publicity duties are well documented within the body of your résumé, you needn't change the copy there (though of course you will play up the publicity angle on your cover pitch).

- If, on the other hand, you've given your role as publicity director short shrift, you should take the time to expand on this in your résumé, too.

Note: In the majority of cases, if you left your job on good terms, your boss will be happy to agree to a slightly revisionist job title. Just make sure you check with bosses before giving out their names as references.

Special Note: If you're currently leaving a job, either because of downsizing, your decision, or "termination," make a mental note to ask your boss to agree to a few different variations on your job title. You might say, "As you know, Dave, it's pretty tough out there, and if I had the freedom to amend my title—only to cover parts of the job I really did—it would be an enormous help." I did this once, and it was a lifesaver—not only in my "real" job search, but in pitching freelance assignments, too.

If At First You Don't Succeed . . .

We've all been there. We see an ad for a job that has our name written all over it, feel fabulous for the rest of the day, write a wondrous pitch letter, wait five days, then don't hear anything at all. Then we get slightly depressed and vow never again to buy another product bearing the name of the company that advertised the job.

Not anymore we don't! Here's the basic problem: In today's economy, an attractive job can draw hundreds and hundreds of responses—sometimes more than 1,000 in large metropolitan areas. So even if you've pitched your heart out and have a résumé to match, there exists the distinct possibility that you've not made it through the first cut.

To cover all your bases, here's what I advise: Send in a duplicate response about ten days after the first. In none but rare instances will the company have hired someone, and your "straggler" response will have much less competition than it did the first time around—thus there's a much better chance you'll be contacted to interview. (Note, please, that this kind of dual approach makes sense only for positions for which you are unequivocally qualified; for anything but a fabulous match, there's probably a good reason the company has elected not to meet with you.)

Similarly, let's say you see the same ad magically reappear a month or two later in the same paper. There are several main reasons this would occur:

1. The company didn't find a perfect match the first time out. Though if this happens for anything but a superspecialized position—one requiring a Ph.D. in Romance Philology, for example—it's probably due to the hiring authority not having a well-developed idea of what he or she wants. (A job's a job, but lemme tell you, folks, my experience has shown this is usually the work of a confused mind, and the kind of person for whom you really don't want to work.)

2. Someone spilled Snapple—accidentally or with vicious intent—over the stack of résumés received. (Alternate

selection: Add your own favorite act of subterfuge—
arson, paper shredding, "misplacement"—here.)

3. The person originally hired is now in jail, rehab, or "didn't work out." (The last category is always great gossip fodder: How can someone not work out after three weeks?)

Whatever the case of the poor man or maid, send in your résumé again. This time, you don't have to wait the requisite five days. The company is probably desperate to find a body for the seat and most people aren't as savvy as you; they'll not send in their résumé one mo' time.

9
•••

Pitching to Recruiters and Search Firms

Of all the elements of a job search, the subject of executive recruiters (lovingly called "headhunters" by one and all) is among the most misunderstood. It follows, therefore, that this valuable resource is also widely misused and maligned by those stalking new jobs.

It's definitely a case of the hunter being captured by the game. Headhunters make their living off the successful placement of candidates, but don't always treat them terribly well. I recall with glee the way my young executive friends and I used to trash the worst offenders whenever we got together. No, we weren't vicious and cruel, but more than a few recruiters were rude, ill mannered, and, sometimes, unethical as hell.

Now, for the good news: Most executive recruiters have a high standard of moral conduct and should be considered your allies, integral to your overall job hunt. If they don't follow up as much as they should and, increasingly, don't even acknowledge the résumé you sent, remember this: We're not in the eighties anymore. Recruiter's profit margins are down, too, and the ratio of super well qualified job seekers to jobs is higher than ever before.

That wasn't always the case. Even ten years ago, many people relied on headhunters to the extent that they became the beginning and end of their new job search. (This was especially true for candidates with excellent credentials and job experience living in or near metropolitan areas.) Someone with, for example, a top MBA in accounting who had worked for only Top Eight firms and had no criminal record or major personality disorders could pretty much count on a recruiter to find him or her a new job in any major city in the United States. (It's still possible, but only the most uninspired or casual job hunter would conduct so lethargic a campaign.)

Which brings us to an important point: Executive recruiters are excellent at matching apples with apples—and, sometimes, yellow apples with red ones. And, to be honest, an elite cadre among them does take the time to explore deeper than a candidate's surface. But don't expect them to carve a new career path for you; that's something you have to do yourself.

A specific example: I was a marketing manager at Revlon's Ultima II division when a headhunter contacted me about a position at Swatch Watch. No, cosmetics and fashion watches are not the same thing; they are, however, both "image" products, distributed in department stores, spend lots of money for fancy advertising, and are a category where ongoing product development, design, and packaging are key. Moreover, companies like Swatch traditionally took people from the cosmetics industry, so there was never a question that the fit would be good.

Consider, on the other hand, the case of Bella Blue (page 99). She was creative, attractive, and smart as a whip, but only the most challenge-loving headhunter would try to place her with a cosmetics firm. Frankly, they don't have to: In today's economy, there are legions of cosmetics marketers who are out of jobs, and neither recruiters nor their clients (companies) have to look outside the industry.

Generally speaking, then, executive recruiters match people in the same industry. If you're very enterprising, however, you can pitch your background to headhunters just as you would a client. But, because this is barking up a fairly unresponsive tree, I advise that you do this only in the following cases:

1. When you've been recommended to a recruiting firm by a friend or directly contacted by the firm.

2. When you know that a certain executive recruiter works in an industry in which you're intensely interested.

For example, Bella could have sent a pitch letter similar to the one she wrote directly to cosmetics companies to recruiters who work in the field. A creative pitch is less likely to work with headhunters than it is with a hiring authority at the company itself, but if you're the type—like me—who can't fall asleep at night until you've covered absolutely every base, you might want to try this tactic. But again: Don't make this the cornerstone of your campaign.

How should you locate executive recruiters in your field? The following rules apply:

1. The easiest and best way: Ask your colleagues and friends in the field. People in your field who have similar backgrounds are very likely to have their own list of re-

cruiters. (It goes without saying that only your intimates and/or acquaintances you can trust implicitly should be asked for headhunters' names!) Also, don't forget to call friends in different cities for their lists, especially if relocation is not a problem for you.

2. Look in the phone book under "Executive Recruiters." True, most firms don't advertise there, but some do. (Again, it's a question of covering every possible base.) Some of you may be querulous about doing this, especially if you're currently employed, but I've never heard of anyone's career being ruined by a headhunter who went and called their boss. At worst, a randomly contacted recruiter won't respond to your letter; I've never met one who was pathologically vitriolic!

3. Consult the *Directory of Executive Recruiters,* the acknowledged Bible in the field. (It's available in the business sections of most large libraries, or write to Kennedy Publications, Templeton Road, Fitzwilliam, NH 03447; or call them at (603) 585-2200.) This reference work is massive and loaded with names, but I find it rather cumbersome to use—as do most people I've ever talked to, who get tired of cross-referencing industries and geographical areas in short order indeed. Another drawback of this is that many search firms bill themselves as working in a given industry or specialty—say, marketing, health care, accounting, etc.—and, in point of fact, haven't made a placement in that area for years (if ever). This is precisely why amassing friends' lists is always the very best way to proceed. Certainly, there may be deadwood there, but you can count on finding far less there than in a guide-compiled list.

4. My secret weapon—the first thing I did when conducting my own job search several years ago—is to call the
Recruiting & Search Report at (800) 634-4548. This
firm offers the most comprehensive and least expensive
headhunter lists known to woman or man, and they're
constantly updated for accuracy's sake. You can order lists
segmented by industry/functional specialty and/or geographical area, and I can't recommend this service highly
enough as a marvelous alternative to combing through
clunky reference guides. A godsend!

So now you have your list. How many names are on it? That
depends on factors like the number of headhunters in your industry—some have scads, others a scant few—and whether or
not you're free to relocate. (If you're limiting yourself to your
immediate environs, your job search will, in general, be a
tough row to hoe.)

Now you're ready to write your letter. Take it easy—this
one's a relative no-brainer. No fancy pitching needed here, just
a clear, concise outline of what you've done. A letter like this:

JOHN LACAMARA
12345 Hunter Drive
Santa Fe, NM 88888
Phone Number Here

Date

Ms. Anita Bookner
Vice President
DeKALB & ASSOCIATES
Alamo Industrial Park #333
Houston, TX 33333

Dear Ms. Bookner:

If a hospital services administrator with ten years' experience in major medical facilities meets the requirements of a current search, please consider me.

Presently, I am patient services director at New Mexico General in Albuquerque; my salary is $60,000.

Among the highlights of my background:

- Patient services and staff administration positions at Boston General, St. Paul Children's, and Wichita Medical Center
- Three citations for superior performance
- At present job, increased patient satisfaction level by 60 percent, per an independently commissioned survey
- MS in Health Administration, George Washington University
- BA in English, University of Maryland

I am fully fluent in English and Spanish.

If my professional qualifications meet a current search need, I would be happy to discuss my background further with you. Thank you.

Sincerely,

John Lacamara

No fancy pitching here, only a straightforward, pithy précis of John's qualifications. The headhunter to whom he has sent his résumé is either working on an assignment that matches John's qualifications, or she isn't.

For this reason, direct mailing to executive recruiters need not be followed up by a call on your part. In fatter times, I remember that New York headhunters, staffed with young associates, would call in top-drawer candidates just to know who they were. Today's leaner environment precludes this, even at the most prestigious firms. In fact, ten years ago, every respectable recruiter would send a card or letter acknowledging receipt of your résumé; few today have the staffing and funds to do so. While it's human nature to consider this rude, executive recruiters need to spend their time in the most lucrative possible way, so don't take it personally.

What you *should* take personally is when you spend half an hour going over your background with a recruiter, either in person or on the phone, then receive no response. My position here is unflappable: Such a one's manners are odious, end of discussion. It's slightly better mannered, but still fairly insulting, to be called by a secretary of the firm if you have spent a goodly amount of time pitching yourself. Someone who can't be bothered to call and/or leave a message such as

"John, I thoroughly enjoyed meeting you, and think your background and attitude are very impressive; unfortunately, our client has decided to pursue candidates with more experience in major metropolitan medical centers."

doesn't deserve the time of day.

Just this week, two of my clients told me of this kind of "Let them eat cake" attitude on the part of two midlevel recruiters on the West Coast. My answer was the same in both cases: Yes, the headhunters acted despicably, but they're in the driver's seat. When you're job-hunting, it's only natural that your nerves be slightly frazzled, but please resist the opportunity to call and tell them off. Letting them have it may be slightly cathartic, but it won't change their substandard business etiquette, and besides, you never know when they might call back.

Oddly enough—maybe because they're totally clueless—it's just these kinds of clods who are the first to call you at your new place of business when you do get a job, pitching their services to you. At that time, you have my full permission to tell them how uncouth they are, and how you can't believe they even had the nerve to pick up the phone. (When you're in the driver's seat, ain't revenge sweet?)

One other, very important note: When it comes to headhunters, if at first you don't succeed, try, try again! If you do get a courtesy "ding" note, it will probably include the classic sentence, "We will keep your materials on file should we begin work on an appropriate search." And indeed, many firms will do just that.

But with thousands of CVs on file, how great is the chance they'll actually dredge yours up, even when they do a key industry search? Out of sight is out of mind; for this reason, I recommend that you resend résumés to your most highly targeted list—i.e., those firms you know to specialize in your field of work—every three months. Unlike ill-advised repeat phone calls, it can't hurt, and, if the firm happens to be working on a relevant search, it could very well help get you a job.

One of the biggest mistakes job hunters make is to treat headhunter-generated interviews as if they were gifts from an alternate universe, with their own set of rules and regulations. Let me ask you this: If you won a car on a game show, as opposed to working your butt off for it, wouldn't you still have to insure it and follow the rules of the road? Of course you would. So your follow-up for interviews in this category should mirror your secondary pitches for job leads you generated on your own.

That means the people you interviewed with on your visit to the company should all receive the kind of "personal pitch thank-you notes" that you'd write regardless of whether a headhunter put you in contact with them or not. There's just one difference: Before spending your time pitching yourself in writing, wait to hear from the headhunter. Unlike most interviews for professional positions, where you can wait weeks to hear something, most headhunters will let you know how things went within several days of the interview. Thus, *if the recruiter reports that things went well, and Company Z is interested in taking things to the next step, you should immediately write thank-yous to every single person you interviewed with.*

Stop thinking about this as work! It's an *opportunity*, one to cement your position with the folks you met. Write even to the people at your own level (or below): The reason you talked to them is because the upper brass respects them enough to get their opinion. Don't try to bowl these people over with your brilliance; the last thing they want is a hotshot who'll outshine them. Instead, let them think they've found a new best friend:

Mr. Bill Chan
Project Director
SUPER SPORTS SHOES
333 Shortsprint Way
Miami, FL 33333

Dear Bill:

Great to meet you during my trip to Miami last week. (I was expecting all business; who knew I'd get to see South Beach's hottest spots as well?)

Though I've been a personal fan of Super Sports' shoes for years, I'm now an equal supporter of your super management team. Everyone I met was incredibly enthusiastic, full of great ideas, and poised for even greater future success. I loved hearing about your department's new products in development—they sound terrific!

Bill, thanks again for showing me around. I hope to be a part of the Miami scene myself very soon.

Best,

James Giannelli

The letter above is perfect when writing to thank someone on or around your own level; it's friendly, upbeat, and to the point, but doesn't run the risk of intimidating potential colleagues with your genius. (It's sad but true that most corporate workers are incredibly insecure, and would do anything to dissuade their boss from hiring an applicant perceived as gifted—someone like you, for instance!)

On the other hand, a follow-up letter to the hiring authority or other chieftains should bellow your brilliance from here to eternity. (Note: if you think that person might be scared of what you have to offer—something I've encountered many times in my career—you're barking up the wrong tree; continue your search until you find a boss who'll accept you for the sharpshooter you are!) A letter like this will work wonders:

Mr. John Trumbull
Chief Operating Officer
SUPER SPORTS SHOES

Dear Mr. Trumbull (or John, if he suggested you call him that during your interview):

Thank you so much for taking the time to meet with me during my visit to your firm. I realize you are extremely busy, and am thus grateful you carved time from your schedule to discuss Super Sports' present activities and future plans.

My immediate impression of your remarkable company is this: Super Sports is committed to producing shoes of high quality at the most advantageous price points, and to introducing tomorrow's styles, today. It is a philosophy that has certainly contributed to your meteoric rise in the footwear field, and one whose wisdom I surely share.

Even more important is my unique professional experience, one which can help take Super Sports Shoes to still-greater heights. Most germane is my five-year role as Product Development Manager for Avenue Shoes, during which time I orchestrated the introduction of AirTops, now the #1 walking shoe brand in the United States. As we discussed, in addition to my design direction, I supervised all phases of the advertising and publicity campaign for these and other shoe lines.

My knowledge of contemporary footwear is matched only by my enthusiasm for your fine company and the many directions in which I know it can expand. I am especially keen on the idea of a children's line, and look forward to presenting my ideas to you at an opportune time.

In the meantime, Mr. Trumbull, thank you again for your interest and time.

Best regards,

James Giannelli

Based on personal experience, I guarantee that James's letter is better than about 95 percent of those I've seen, and it certainly represents a great pitch. But it's not, in the strictest sense, a Perfect Pitch, and I'm sure you can guess why. That's right: the textbook Perfect Pitch would not merely allude to, but would actually include, anything from highly-targeted suggestions for future growth to a fully fleshed-out business plan (the kind I wrote to get my job at Revlon when I was making the move from another, only marginally related, field). Too much work, you say? That's your choice, my friend; as I've said repeatedly, Perfect Pitching requires work, and more often than not, it's the most convincing candidate who gets the job.

The caveat to this is when your interview with the hiring authority (or other big shots) didn't go especially well. In this case, it's not inconceivable that a wildly winning follow-up pitch could get you a job but, to be honest, it's rare. If a hiring authority just doesn't click with you, or for whatever other reason feels you're not right for the company's team, don't bark up the wrong tree; turn your attention to greener, more welcoming pastures. (Arboreal images are obviously not *my* specialty, so I'll take my own advice and cease and desist from using them henceforth!)

If the headhunter calls to tell you that you're not quite the hiring company's cup of tea (insert your favorite apologia here), you have several choices:

1. If you agree the fit wasn't right, you hated the city or headquarters/product line/staff, erase the entire episode from your memory; don't bother with a thank-you note. (A friend of mine had me in stitches after an ill-fated trip to a computer company in a desolate industrial part

on the wrong side of the San Francisco Bay, the high-light of which was lunch bought off a mobile taco stand and eaten *standing up.* "Call me a snob," she sniffed, "but I didn't make it from Fresno to Stanford to eat lunch off a truck!")

2. If you're given the high hat via a recruiter, but are dying to work for the company and think you have something to offer, write follow-up pitch notes to your contact and the highest-ranking person you met. I suggest something like this:

> Ms. Laura Tijera
> President
> SUPER SPORTS SHOES
> 333 Shortsprint Way
> Miami, FL 33333
>
> Dear Laura (or Ms. Tijera if you stand on ceremony):
>
> Having read so many articles citing your accomplishments while doing my research, I was happy to finally meet the woman herself. Thanks ever so much for taking the time to meet with me during my round of interviews in Miami.
>
> While I understand from Hank Hennessey that you have elected not to pursue my candidacy at this time, I wanted to let you know how interested I am in joining Super Sports' design [or marketing or accounting or sales] team. Though I understand your hesitancy given my lack of shoe design experience, I do believe that my proven record in clothing design—abetted by a burning

desire to work in your product category—would allow me to make significant contributions to your company's ongoing success.

I've taken the liberty of enclosing a couple of sketches I made after discussing your new children's line with Bill Chan. When there's a will, there's a way; maybe I'll fit into your company's future plans.

In the meantime, Laura, thanks again for your kindness. Onward and upward for Super Sports Shoes!

Best,

James Giannelli

Will James's extra efforts pay off? In the immediate time frame, probably not. However, as I told you before, I have seen a previously rejected candidate be called back on more than one occasion because the person they hired: (a) turned down the job after accepting it; (b) was a great interview but a lousy employee; (c) decided the job wasn't for him or her after coming on board.

This very situation happened to me once. I had gone through a grueling set of interviews with a prestigious cosmetics company over a period of several months. At the end point, the position of marketing director was a toss-up between me and one other person. Ultimately, the president of the division decided, all other things being equal, he'd rather have a woman in the spot. I was crushed, but wrote stunning thank-you notes on my best Brooks Brothers stationery. (At the time, I thought my whole career would be as a cosmetics executive—how narrow are our horizons at age twenty-six!—and wanted to look like the classiest guy ever in their eyes.)

Shortly thereafter, I accepted a position with Swatch Watch (not a bad consolation prize). About four months into my tenure there, I came home to find a message on my home answering machine from the human resources director at the cosmetics company, informing me that the person they hired was pregnant and decided she didn't want to work any longer. Would I be interested in reactivating my application? I surely would have been, had I not already taken a position. The moral of the story is, I think, quite clear: Don't close the door on anyone or anything.

I'll not lead you down the primrose path; the likelihood of this happening, or even being reconsidered after an initial "ding," is slim. If you have anything less than an overwhelming desire to work for a certain firm (if, for example, they're in your all-time top ten) and/or are working on a lot of different angles, it may not be worth it to you to bend over backwards this way.

In James's case, even if Laura Tijera had not been swayed by his fabulous sketches, she immediately becomes a name on his target list. (Note: If there is absolutely no chemistry between you and the hiring authority, don't beat a dead horse. If, on the other hand, you sense a rapport and respect of your skills, but just didn't fit their specifications to a T, the door is still open for the future.) Given that Super Sports Shoes is a fast-growing firm, he can pitch her again in several months' time. That provides enough courtesy time for the recruiter, and also allows for the possibility of new opportunities having cropped up at that firm.

10

• • •

Pitching to Employment Agencies

"Okay," I hear you concede, "I understand why it's important to pitch to high-level executive recruiters. But I'm looking for an entry-level or administrative job. Can pitching really work at my level?"

Of course it can! In several important ways:

1. *In your initial contact.* Most job seekers simply send (or, increasingly, fax) their résumés without a cover note—totally pitchless, as it were. By using the very same pitching principles covered in the previous chapter on headhunters, you can exponentially increase your visibility—and, consequently, your professionalism—with employment agencies.

2. *In your personal contacts with the agency.* Surprisingly, many job hunters visit personnel agencies, take the obligatory battery of tests, and meet with counselors without having a firm idea of what they want to do. So it's little wonder they end up being steered into

any available job and taking the first one offered to them.

We've already seen in Chapter 5, however, how the Perfect Pitcher always knows what he or she is going after. The goal here is simple: make employment agencies work for you. Know exactly what industries the firm has as clients; if there are none in your target category, there's no point in wasting your time with typing and spelling tests (or, for that matter, the obligatory dry-cleaning bill). You're interviewing the agency as much as it's interviewing you. (The same principle holds for those investigating temporary employment; see Chapter 11).

3. *In your meetings with potential employers.* Every single tenet of the Perfect Pitch holds equally true for job leads generated by employment agencies as for those generated by any other technique. With one exception: your initial hookup, which will have been effected by the agency rather than networking or a résumé submission initiated by you. For this reason, your personal interview and follow-up communications become the areas in which you can pitch to win. (My comments regarding post-interview follow-up with agency-generated hiring authorities mirror those for headhunter-effected meetings; refer to page 113 as a refresher course.)

Here are key tips to keep in mind when using employment agencies as part of your job campaign:

• Always register with several to keep your bases covered— and more if you live in a large metropolitan area. But don't register indiscriminately! Friends' and associates' recommendations are always the best way to find agencies in your area that have good reputations not only for placements but for treating applicants with courtesy and integrity.

• Depending on your professional aspirations, the company and its industry may not be important to you. For instance, if you're looking for a post as an executive secretary, the salary and responsibilities may be your prime goal. If, however, you're using agencies as an entry-level stepping-stone within your chosen career, make sure an agency actually has clients in that area before wasting your time with the tests and interviews.

• If you're looking for a managerial position that pays between $30,000 and $75,000 (a salary usually too low to be of interest to executive recruiters), make sure to go after firms specializing in your area and not agencies that deal mainly with secretaries and assistants. In addition to your colleagues' recommendations, you can contact the following organization:

National Association of Personnel Consultants
1432 Duke Street
Alexandria, VA 22314
(703) 684-0180

The NAPC publishes a national directory of employment agencies, along with their professional specialties and geographic locations.

• If the agency asks you to sign a contract, read it very carefully. If it contains rules and regulations regarding each party's responsibilities, codes of conduct, and non-competitive clauses, that's fine; if it asks you to commit to some financial fee, drop it like a hot potato. Fees are always paid by the client company, not you.

- Similarly, if you feel pressured or in any way uncomfortable with the counselor to whom you have been assigned, you need feel no compunction about electing not to work with that firm. The great majority of employment agencies are above board and treat candidates with respect; if, however, you feel anxious about a given firm's operating tactics, don't hesitate to move on.

- Establish rapport with your agency counselor, and you're in the inside circle. If there are one or two counselors with whom you're able to strike up a personal relationship, so much the better; they'll work like blazes to get you placed. In any case, follow-up letters—not just thank-you notes, but bona fide pitches—can work wonders. Why? Because, quite simply, most of your competition won't have the class to do so. Use this as your opportunity to state and restate your job goals and as a "point of difference" to become memorable in your counselors' eyes.

If you've got a very specific goal, try a letter like this:

Ms. Dinah Jenkins
ABC Personnel, Inc.
333 Renaissance Center
Detroit, MI 33333

Dear Dinah:

Meeting you today was a great pleasure indeed.

I'm delighted that your agency has working contacts in the automotive industry, which, as we discussed, is my ultimate goal. I believe that my associate's degree in business, organizational skills, and status as an amateur mechanic would place me in good stead with any one of the Big Three.

To that end, I'm willing to wait until the appropriate job in "the industry" comes up, and will contact you every three weeks as you asked. In the meantime, Dinah, great to meet you, and thanks for thinking of me.

Best regards,

Anthony DiCicco

Simple and to the point, Anthony's letter serves to keep him on top of Dinah's mind—and also positions him as a class act. You can be sure that Dinah will think of him first when the appropriate position crops up.

Of course, the principles of Perfect Pitching apply once you've met with a company for which you'd like to work. A note reaffirming your interest and capabilities (like the one on pages 113–114) should be written and mailed on the day of the interview wherever possible.

Finally, it's always a good idea to keep in constant contact with counselors you respect (and agencies with lots of work). While you shouldn't beleaguer them with phone calls, a follow-up note is always a nice touch:

Ms. Melinda Gammon
Midwest Careers
777 Cornhusk Way
Lincoln, NE 68588

Dear Melinda:

Just a follow-up note to fill you in on my meeting with Anton Gorchin at Tractors Unlimited.

While I enjoyed our meeting, I think we both felt that my experience was not quite right for his current needs. Anton is looking for a right-hand person who also offers considerable experience in accounting, which is not really my field. I'm sure he'll find someone wonderful, and of course I asked him to keep me in mind should a better fit for me crop up at his firm (pardon the pun!).

Once again, Melinda, thank you for thinking of me. I'm sure we'll find the perfect fit very soon.

Best,

JoJo Brachman

Are you one step ahead of me? Good! Then you know what I'm thinking: If JoJo hit it off with Anton and had her heart set on joining his firm, she'd write him a follow-up pitch, too. (Refer to the letter on page 117 for a strong example of continuing your pitch with your A-list, even if you've been rejected once.)

11
. . .

Temporary Solutions

I love temporary workers. At Revlon, I inherited (along with a closetful of lipsticks from the 1940s) a wonderful free spirit named Butterfly who split her time between a rent-controlled Lower East Side apartment, her "house" in Majorca, and various other points twixt here and Mars. She claimed to have an MA in art history and to have slept with three of the Rolling Stones.

I found her enchanting, gypsy jewelry and all. (Stevie Nicks had nothing on our Butterfly girl.) When I asked, in my naively nose-to-the-grindstone way, how she could live a life devoid of apparent security, she answered, "Life, my darling, is for living." That was just before she blew off for Australia with a bagful of "borrowed" blushers I'm sure she sold on the beach.

I, too, am an alumnus of that glorious fraternity known as temping. And I, like many dedicated temps, have been offered a permanent position at nearly every gig I ever had. Here's the good news: You can be, too.

Until very recently, temps were viewed suspiciously by workers in the on-staff world—mysterious figures with checkered pasts who (obviously, or why would they be temping?) couldn't get a "real" job. We temps were whispered about in the shadows of watercoolers and mammoth Xerox machines, no doubt thought to be one small step above child molesters, drug dealers, and pimps. (Or *were* we one or more of the above; who knew?)

Those days, thankfully, are long gone. With the downsizing (or, euphemistically, "rightsizing") of corporate America, more and more workers—from mail clerks to professionals with advanced degrees—are working the temp game. And the more astute among them are making this temporary status (pardon the pun) work for them.

The upside, then, is that temps are no longer marginal figures to be shunned by decent folk. The downside is that, except for the most committed bohemians (like Butterfly), a lifetime of temporary employment can be far more terrifying than fun.

Indeed, as G. J. Meyer writes in his poignant memoir, *Executive Blues: Down and Out in Corporate America*:

> *Organizational gurus have been writing and lecturing about how the corporation of the not-very-distant future will have only a tiny, almost vestigial permanent staff. This corporation will meet most of its needs for white-collar work by hiring outsiders temporarily, project by project. . . .*

Meyer goes on to disparage the Pollyanna-ish attitude of our more upbeat theorists, who adopt a sort of postcapitalist ardor for our collective newfound freedom. For every Butterfly, Meyer rightly contends, there are a thousand more typical folks who relish being able to sleep at night knowing they have a job to come to in the morning—as well as such attendant luxuries as health insurance and retirement plans. Or, as the *New York Times* so pithily put it in an acclaimed seven-part series on downsizing, ". . . [The] old certainties about work no longer apply."

How far the situation of "transitional" workers can devolve without pushing the masses to revolt is anyone's guess. Happily, according to my man Mario Cuomo in his wonderful book, *Reason to Believe,* "Indeed, there is some evidence that the entire downsizing syndrome may have passed the point of diminishing returns, producing what has been called 'corporate anorexia.' " If this is the case, it augurs well for large-scale restaffing, a trend one can but hope to be long-lived.

In the meantime, using temporary work to your advantage is the name of the game. Two main categories of "temping" apply:

Temporary Work as a Stopgap Measure

The stigma of temp assignments long since having been cast aside, you should embrace the temporary world as your personal invitation to a limitless universe of new kinds of work. I've been there and done that, and have had some wonderful experiences as a temp. Among my favorites:

- As secretary to the publisher of *Working Woman* Magazine, I had about two hours of work every day, and spent the rest of the time looking for a full-time job. (This was summer in New York City, and I would've paid *them* for the air-conditioned bliss.) A fledgling writer, I sent my rather meager credentials—wrapped up in a full-blown pitch—to the managing editor and was awarded a monthly column, "Just for You"! ("I'm obviously not the magazine's target audience," I wrote, "but as a staffer in your advertising department, I know your reader's demographic profile like nobody else.") I still keep this item on my writing résumé as a conversation piece.

- After Revlon was bought out and I lost my job, I got a temporary assignment at Shiseido, the Japanese cosmetics firm. This soon became a consultancy, and might well have led to a full-time job if I hadn't got another one before they could make an offer.

Still unconvinced? How about these tales of success:

- Michele B., my assistant at New Line Cinema (remember her from this book's introduction?), who is now a highly regarded marketing director.

- Tommy I., a current client, whose knowledge of Spanish was able to transform a "nothing" temp spot at Avon into a six-month-long stint in their Hispanic Products Division. (He's now pitching himself—with promising early results—as a publicity coordinator for other major cosmetics and fashion firms.)

So temporary positions can lead to permanent work—and, when engineered correctly, to the job of your dreams. Here is the inside scoop on how to really maximize your prospects and open the window of opportunity as far as it will go.

1. Find the Best Temporary Agencies in Your Area, and Let Them Work for You

Ask Your Friends

They're always the best source of referrals for temporary agencies, executive recruiters, personnel agencies, and the like. (It goes without saying that by "friends" I mean your entire circle of intimates, acquaintances, and co-workers—anyone who can give you good leads.)

Consult the Phone Book

Virtually every temporary agency in town will have a listing in the Yellow Pages under "Temporary Employment" or "Temporary Services." While the big names everyone knows—like Olsten and Manpower—are uniformly excellent and known for their top-notch treatment of client companies and temporaries both, don't be afraid of the smaller "boutique" concerns. This is especially true in big cities like Los Angeles, where two or three temp agencies specialize in the entertainment industry—the kind of company practically everyone here wants to break into. Similarly, smaller agencies in your local area may specialize in banking, the medical industry, or other fields.

Register with Several Agencies

More important, compare their rates, the kinds of firms (prestige vs. schlock) they send their people to, and the level of professionalism and kindness of their "counselors." (These are the folks who send you into the wild unknown of tempdom.)

Tell the Counselor(s) Where You Want to Be

When you first start out, you're nowhere near the driver's seat. Still, you should pleasantly advise your counselor in which industries you'd most like to work. At the best temp agencies, your counselor will do his or her best to accommodate your wishes.

Tell Your Counselor Again after You've Worked a Couple of Jobs with Their Agency

If you've completed several assignments with a given firm (or firms) and know your work was respected, you're now a valuable commodity at that firm. Call your counselor and tell him or her how much you enjoy representing their company, and remind him or her of your interest in the publishing/advertising/consumer products, etc., world. Temporary workers with good skills, nice appearances, a strong work ethic, and engaging personalities are the agencies' stock-in-trade. After you've proved your mettle, use it for all it's worth!

Better yet, write a letter and tell them how you really feel. A pitch like this would be just perfect:

Ms. Rachel Lavine
TempsPlus, Inc.
45 Greenwich Avenue
New York, NY 10000

Dear Rachel:

I'm just finishing up my three-week assignment with the law offices of Robinson, Raines & Riboux, and wanted to thank you for sending me here. The people are all lovely, and I think I've picked up enough law to start my own firm!

But, as you know, Rachel, the world of TV is where it's at for me. (You'll remember I told you I majored in broadcasting at Syracuse.) So, my dear, please keep your eyes and ears open for temp assignments at one of the networks or cable companies. (Frieda in your office told me that ABC, CBS, and Showtime are all clients of your firm's.)

Thanks again, Rachel; working for TempsPlus (and with you!) is always a joy.

Best,

Shelley Kowalski

How many people take this kind of initiative? I think you know the answer: precious few. Most people let their careers happen to them; smart pitchers like Shelley know that it's up to them, not the gods, to get what they want. (A letter like the one above not only brings her closer to a TV network, but cements her position as a top temp with her firm. Because she's seen as a woman of worth—and, yes, class—you can be sure that Shelley will be at the top of her counselor's list for the most plum assignments when they come in.)

2. Once You Get Your Foot in Your Target Industry, Work that Temp Job like There's No Tomorrow!

For some lucky people, temp assignments naturally evolve into full-time careers. But you're too smart to rely on luck: Grab the situation by the reins and make it work for you. Here's how:

(a) If you're on a long-term assignment, do a fabulous job during the first few weeks, and wait for your bosses and colleagues to fall in love with you. In addition to performing your duties with élan, don't cower in the corner (a mistake most temps make); act like you're working there full-time. It all depends on the specific situation, of course; some companies have cliques as firmly entrenched as in high school; others have more fluid staffs, and making friends will be far easier here. Invite your co-workers to lunch; make every effort to get under their (and their bosses') skins.

(b) Once you've shown how terrific you are, go to your boss at an opportune time (Friday afternoon or when they look to be in a great mood are best) and tell him or her something about yourself.

A verbal pitch like this can work wonders:

"Joan, may I have a word with you?"

(Chances are, you'll be met with a smile and the reply, "Of course"; but if Joanie changes into her dragon lady phase, say, "Later might be better" and run like the wind.)

"Joan, I've been here for three weeks now, and I've enjoyed my work here immensely . . . and I hope you've been equally pleased with me."

(In all probability, you'll be the subject of return compliments; remember, you're only going to approach people you know like you and your work.)

"I wanted to have a word with you, because even though you know me as a 'temp,' I actually have a degree in broadcasting from Syracuse, and am interested in exploring career possibilities with CBS. My area of concentration is news editorial, but of course I'm not limiting myself to that area. And it goes without saying that I'm more than willing to pay my dues. But I wanted to ask if you'd be kind enough to help me get a foot in the door of that division of CBS."

Joan's reaction will range from extremely solicitous to noncommittal; it depends entirely on the kind of person she is. Many people love helping others; making a couple of phone calls or directing your résumé somewhere requires a minimum of effort, but can be an immense boost to the person across the desk. I myself believe in karma—have I been living in California too long?—and do whatever I can, sometimes for people I barely know. On the other hand, I've asked good friends to help me, and have got the cold shoulder, but good—and sometimes even outright indignance at how I could have the gall to ask for help. When people fall into this category, they're either jealous of your abilities, genuine miscreants, or were of the silver spoon born, and can't comprehend why you'd need their help. The bottom line, though, is that most people are only too happy to do what they can. But when they're not, don't beg: It won't work with people like that, and you're better than they are anyway.

(c) Follow up with the company's personnel department, either clerical or executive departments. Depending on your relationship (if any) with these people, pitch on the phone—or, better yet, in writing—advising them how much you've enjoyed working there, and letting them know of your long-range plans. Secure a meeting with the appropriate personnel staffer and pitch your heart out. Always leave the meeting with a clear vision of how to proceed, and where to look for jobs within the firm. Does the company have posted job listings? Is a newsletter circulated? Or do you have to keep in constant contact with Personnel? Whatever the permutations of the above, keep yourself—and your abilities— at the top of their minds.

3. Contact Large Firms in Your Area Directly

Many people don't realize that most large companies have their own reserve temporary staff. Often called "floaters," these people comprise career temps (like our pal Butterfly, working mothers, would-be actors, etc.), as well as men and women who use these positions as a springboard to the job of their dreams. Your mission becomes clear: Simply call the personnel office of companies in your target industry and ask if they have a bank of in-house temps; if so, how can you apply for this corps? I can't begin to tell you how many people I've advised who have used this technique to gain permanent employment in the field of their choice. Just think about it: Wouldn't an employer rather hire someone whose work they know when a permanent position becomes available than start the hiring process from the beginning?

Working as a temp—one employed by either an agency or a target company itself—is a technique I'm especially quick to advise for liberal arts graduates who want to infiltrate certain "glamour fields" like entertainment, publishing, cosmetics, and the media—industries where almost everyone has to start from the ground up (with the exception of people with advanced degrees in areas like finance and law). Estée Lauder and Columbia Pictures are two prestigious, sought-after companies with in-house temp programs that spring immediately to mind.

Professional Temporary Work

Twenty years ago, the lion's share of temporary assignments was for clerical personnel and laborers. Today, the phenomenon of downsizing has created a huge new arena of temporary help: professionals in myriad fields. In fact, about 40 percent of all temps are people in a wide range of professional and technical fields. From nurses to engineers, accountants to chemists, companies are looking for temporary help to augment their "regular" staff.

How to find agencies that place temps in your field? Here are a few suggestions:

1. *Call your colleagues.* Your trusted friends and co-workers are the best sources here; they may have been contacted

by (or worked for) temporary agencies in the profession you share.

2. *Consult the Yellow Pages.* As stated above, any temp agency of merit will have a listing—and better yet, a display ad—there.

3. *Call the local or national headquarters of trade organizations in your field.* These associations will certainly know of temp placement agencies; just don't take "I don't know" for an answer from the person who answers the phone. Dig and delve, and the answer will be yours. (The person in charge of public relations for the organization is your best bet; even if he or she doesn't know of any temp agencies, he or she will know whom you should call.)

4. *If none of the above techniques yield results, call the National Association of Temporary Services at (703) 549-6287.* They will know beyond a doubt whether a temp agency in your field does business where you live and work.

12
...

Pitching for Promotions...
Or Keeping the Job
You Have

Face it: Whether you're in your first job or have been in the workforce for decades, there are people of whom you've been jealous as hell.

We all know who they are: the golden boys and girls who advance to dizzying job career heights with the greatest of ease, who are quoted in trade publications and the national press, who fly around the world first-class to glitter and glow while everyone else stays behind and does the work.

Oh sure, some of them are the Tori Spellings and John-John Kennedys and Princess Stephanies I used as examples in the beginning of this book. And if you watch enough TV movies, you'll begin to believe that everyone in high-profile industries is sleeping their way to the top.

Some people, of course, are doing just that. In fact, my vitriolic roman à clef about the underbelly of the cosmetics world was rejected by several publishers for being "too tawdry; nobody'd believe that stuff really goes on." (How naïve they were—I'd saved the really juicy parts for the second book!)

But the vast, overwhelming ocean of bodies out there in the workaday world are neither sleeping with their boss(es) nor to the manner born. Moreover, you know it's not just the superbrains who make it to the top of the corporate heap: Who can't count the times we've seen lesser souls rise to the top?

No, it's not necessarily the *best* who boast meteoric careers; it is, however, the *brightest*. Not bright in the schoolbook sense, but bright as in stars: effervescent, glowing, visible from galaxies away. I sat in awe for many a year watching people who were less creative, educated, and results-oriented than I pass me by until I decided that I was every bit as good as they were— nay, better!—and the world should know it. Thus began my odyssey to find my Personal Perfect Pitch.

And you can find yours, too. But know this, and know it well: Pitching yourself is something you do day in and day out, not once in a while. It's a long-term mind-set, if you like, and it's the one quality shared by everyone who's brilliantly successful in their field. Madonna, Bill Clinton, Janet Jackson, Quentin Tarantino, Judith Krantz: Regardless of the quality of their work, all have constantly pitched themselves to the American (and international) public time and time again. When their success became astronomical, of course, they had other people— publicists, admen, campaign specialists—pitching them, but remember this: *At the beginning, the only person who's going to pitch you is yourself.*

So let's get to work. These steps to the Personal Perfect Pitch are the secrets I've shared only with my clients—until now. Learn them, learn them well, and profit from these for the rest of your professional life!

Your Personal Perfect Pitch

Strut Your Stuff!

Why? Because until you become Madonna or Michael, no one's gonna do it for you. I'm constantly amazed by how little senior execs know who does what in their organizations. In fact, it's astonishing how in the dark most bosses are about the specific duties of people who work for them. So let them know. Broadcast your achievements and give them the prominence they deserve. Two main strategies apply:

Air Your Accomplishments as They Occur

Write memos to your boss to inform him or her of successfully completed assignments, new ideas, the results of tests, etc. Each industry is different, but whether you're in the profit, not-for-profit, or educational arena, there are yardsticks of achievements well known to you.

Be sure to "cc" your boss's boss and other key colleagues, too. This can be tricky: Every organization has its own unwritten code of interlevel contact, and it may take you a while to figure out what to do. If you've got a "good" boss, you might well clear your actions with him or her before proceeding. If you've got a "bad" boss, as I have on more occasions than I care to mention, you might ultimately choose to "cc" his or her boss without asking and run the risk of incurring your boss's wrath. Doing precisely this—letting my boss's boss know of my achievements—ultimately saved my job when my boss tried to go the way of Machiavelli on me.

Write and Circulate Monthly Status Reports

In some companies and jobs, these are mandatory. At Revlon, for instance, I loved writing these; they became my own personal stage, one from which I pitched like a pro—and always ended up sounding like much more of a winner than other people at my level. If status reports aren't mandatory, so much the better. You'll have no competition and that much more room to shine. Extra added bonus: If your boss ever tries to fire you, you'll have a great arm in your arsenal and can multiply your severance package or right to transfer to another job in the firm.

Even if you are in a company where other people submit status reports, you've still got a super opportunity to be the star of the show. That's because most people haven't a clue as to how to present even their own accomplishments in the best possible light. You, however, will use this occasion to showcase not only your achievements, but yourself—*pitching* yourself to the powers that be.

Let's say you're a sales representative in the gift industry. (I choose this example because sales professionals almost always have to submit monthly reports to their managers.) Most of your colleagues' status reports will look something like this:

MONTHLY SALES REPORT
November 1997
Alice N. LeRoux

The following details monthly sales activities for subject period.

Existing Accounts

- $5,000 order for each of five Susie's Hallmark stores
- Placed fixtures in 3 Macy's branches; order to be approved for next month.

- Approved $7,500 in returns for Gifts to Go for Xmas merchandise that didn't sell.
- Approved $25,000 co-op advertising payment for Toys and Us; ads to run in May.

New Accounts

- Opened three new gift shops in desert area; total order $14,350.
- Prospected additional stores, but our minimum opening order is too high; therefore, these will be impossible to open at this time.

Ho hum. Alice's report isn't horrible—save for the last, negativistic remark—but it's far from a sales pro's dream. And it certainly won't mark her as a sales rep with energy, vigor, and a positive, "can-do" attitude.

Here's what Alice could have written to make a Perfect Pitch:

MONTHLY SALES REPORT
November 1997
Alice N. LeRoux

Great things continued to happen for Ginza Gifts this month in the southern California sales region! I placed several major holiday orders with existing accounts, put into place a TV ad program that will benefit sales goals regionwide, and continued our company's retail presence in the desert area (the fastest-growing pocket of population in the Southland).

Here's the scoop:

Existing Accounts

- Susie's Hallmark, my #1 independent chain, upped the ante still farther, with their largest per-store order yet. (The local ad program we developed for Valentine's Day really did the trick!)

- Macy's buyer, Diane Raines, finally approved plans for new fixturing—I'm shooting for a $10,000 order per branch to fill the shelves.

- Approved, with Dale Washington's agreement, a $7,500 return for Gifts to Go (unsold holiday items)—with the understanding of a $10,000 order for each store next month.

- Toys and Us has agreed to our terms for a $25,000 co-op advertising program to run next month. All of our SoCal retail accounts are thrilled, as it will surely increase demand in their stores for our products. (As soon as air dates are finalized, I'm sending a letter to all accounts, then plan to follow up for ORDERS!).

New Accounts

- The new leads I generated last month really paid off: three new accounts in the desert. We've now got enough stores there to warrant a small newspaper advertising program; will powwow with Dale to make this happen!

- Five other stores in outlying regions are dying to have our line, but the population density is too low to warrant our current order minimum. Can we discuss ways to waive this amount to increase our presence in these outlying regions? (I'm sure my Midwest colleagues would be happy to support this change.)

There's a world of difference between the two versions of this monthly sales report. One does Alice no favors; at best, it presents her achievements in a staccato, unimpressive fashion. The second version, however, makes her sound like the kind of sales professional her bosses will love: upbeat, forward-minded, ready to turn a challenge into positive results.

Does this approach take more work than the usual sales report, one that's scribbled off in five minutes? Of course it does. But the Perfect Pitcher knows that the rewards of this activity are multifold compared to the extra effort required not merely to report, but to pitch.

Just today, I had lunch with an old friend—currently unemployed—who told me, with more than a twinge of jealousy, about a former colleague he worked with in the international division of a motion picture studio. This person had been the regional marketing chief of a banana republic—a virtual Siberia to fast-track types. "You should have seen his progress reports," my friend confided. "He made everything he did sound so impressive and grand, even though he was stationed in this Third World backwater. And the head of International thought he was the hottest thing since cream cheese. So today," my friend continued, "I just learned he's the head of all operations for the studio in France! Can you believe it?"

Yes, I can—in fact, I'd like to shake this guy's hand. He had his Personal Perfect Pitch down flat!

My friend's diatribe wasn't over. "I mean, David, my region's annual revenues were almost one hundred times what his were. How come he's in France and I'm out on the street?"

"Well, John, why didn't you promote yourself the same way?" I asked.

"Oh, come on, David. I don't have to resort to such brash behavior—I'm a Harvard man. This guy didn't even have an MBA, and I'm sure his degree is from some dustbowl State U."

"That's quite possible. But you're wrong on one count: Harvard or not, in today's environment, you do have to tell the world how good you are. Just *being* good isn't enough."

"But you know me, David. I'm the original Connecticut Yankee. I was raised to think blowing your horn was cheap and shrill."

"Guess what, my friend—so was I. But I learned very early on, it's not just *what* you do, it's *what people think* you're doing. I can't tell you how many people I've worked with in the corporate world who were altogether average, yet who enjoyed meteoric rises because they knew how to shout their achievements—however meager they might be—to the world."

While my friend couldn't help but agree with me, I still don't know if he was convinced vis-à-vis his own career. Indeed, he and I are the last vestiges of that generation where a prestige degree spoke volumes—in most fields, one wasn't bound to promote one's achievements. Today, for better or worse, that world is gone, and no matter who you are and what you do, keeping your achievements in the limelight—*pitching* them, as it were—is absolutely key.

Contribute to Your Company's Monthly Newsletter

Virtually every large organization has an internal news vehicle of some kind. Don't wait for someone to come to you—that won't happen in this lifetime. (And making the newsletter by getting married or having a baby doesn't count as a pitch!)

Look at the various sections of the newsletter and think of ways you can contribute. As someone who has himself edited one of these publications, I can tell you firsthand that getting submissions is like pulling teeth. Editors will be delighted that you're willing to share your point of view. If you're especially industrious, you can (with precious little effort) develop a regular column, such as "Accounting Achievements," "Fresh from Finance," "Contracting Corner," etc., for personal exposure month after month.

Write for Trade Magazines

You say you're not a writer? Doesn't matter. As long as you can construct reasonably intelligent sentences and have a strong point of view, editors of trade magazines—nearly every industry has several, some quite a few—will be your new best friend. They, too, are usually understaffed, hard-pressed to come up with truly interesting new ideas for every new issue, and welcome submissions from people in the business.

Look through the publication, see what kind of stories they run, then come up with a few ideas of your own. Write a letter—yes, a pitch letter—to the editor-in-chief, presenting your credentials as well as story ideas. Don't wait for a response; call him or her to underscore your interest.

Don't be afraid that you have to turn into some kind of journalistic marvel to have your stories see the light of day. A typical article submission can be as short as two typed pages; supplemented with a photograph, it turns into a whole magazine page quite fast.

The happy side benefit of all this is that you become an instant authority in your field. The natural progression is that the trade for which you are writing—and its competitors—will begin to call you for quotes on other stories they run. Voilà! In a matter of months, you can become a resident expert on one or more areas of your industry.

Speak Up!

You don't have to tell me: For most of us, speaking in front of an audience is no fun. Learning to do it, however, increases your visibility exponentially within your company and in your field as a whole. You can deliver your own words of wisdom at:

1. Annual sales meetings
2. Departmental conferences
3. Industry associations
4. Trade shows
5. Anywhere else you're sure to be seen by your colleagues and/or the powers that be

Public speaking is optional, at least until you rise to senior positions within virtually any organization, at which point it becomes de rigueur. Many a junior-level employee has used this arena to propel his or her career growth; if you've got something to say and/or are just a little bit of a ham, you should, too.

Special Pitching Tip: By this stage of the book, I would hope you're one step ahead of me. Use clipped trade magazine articles when you're pitching for promotions, raises, and—of course—new jobs. A copy of one or two articles (more would be overkill) should certainly accompany a pitch letter and résumé when you're investigating jobs within your industry. It automatically positions you as a mover and shaker—just the kind of employee everyone wants to have.

You can also enclose a copy of articles to headhunters who specialize in your field or to whom you have been introduced—that is, a specially selected group of recruiters who you think would actually take the time to give the stories even a short look. Sending them out en masse makes no sense as they probably won't get past the research associate who screens résumés—and who wants to kill trees (and spend a fortune for postage) for naught?

13
• • •

Pitching to Change Careers

By now you understand how effective pitching can be in getting the job you want. Now, know this: If you are actively seeking to change your career, or guide it to even a slightly different plane, finding your Perfect Pitch is an essential tool. Without an absolutely superior pitch, making the move will remain nothing more than a good idea somewhere in the back of your mind.

I've said it before and I'll say it again: When you're looking for a position that's almost exactly the same as the one you currently have, pitching isn't absolutely mandatory, at least not in theory. (I say "not in theory" because in reality, the intense competition in the marketplace usually requires that you outpitch others who are in exactly the same field and position, too.) But to steer your career into new directions, a Perfect Pitch is critical.

The questions, no matter what you're doing now and what your goal(s) may be, are always the same:

What can I say to make my target want to see me?

What specifically do I have to bring to the party that no one else does?

How can I pitch myself in a way that practically dares my target audience not to see me?

Before you can even begin to answer these questions, you must devise the reasons for your Perfect Pitch yourself. There's only one way to begin doing this: to know everything there is to know about your target job and what you have to offer potential employers in the field.

As a career counselor, I am frankly astonished at how little research people do about their target industries, and how little they know about the day-to-day realities of their target jobs. Now, I'm not just talking recent high school and college graduates, whose lack of experience in the workplace can forgive a thousand sins (though the more sophisticated among you will have done your career homework long before putting on that cap and gown); I'm referring here to grown men and women whose dreams of career change, without a fundamental knowledge of their target jobs, are nothing more than old pipe dreams. As Diana Ross sang in *Mahogany*, the debacle that destroyed her film career: "Do you know where you're goin' to?"

Here's my advice, kids: You'd better! Because today's downsized big companies—not to mention energetic, entrepreneurial young firms—have no room for deadwood. Exploratory interviews are, to a large extent, luxuries of the past; to secure an interview, you've got to be dead sure of what you can offer a prospective employer in light of their own staffing needs.

What you want doesn't count a whit. What you can do for the company (or organization or school or hospital) is everything. You've already seen this in the chapter on like-like pitching; multiply this a thousandfold to determine this statement's importance in carving out new careers.

Pitching to expand your professional horizon, once the domain of the exceptionally far-sighted and ambitious, is now a reality we all must share. Truth be told, the reality may be that it's no longer possible to do what you've always done—or what you've always dreamed of doing. My own first dream was to get a Ph.D. in French and teach at a university of the first rank. But the more I explored job prospects in this academic field, I saw that not only was it highly unlikely that I'd end up teaching at a prestigious school, I might find no position at all—or locate a post as an assistant professor, only to be out on my ass the next year. (I have a friend with a Ph.D. in Spanish from Harvard who spent years as a temp, then finally found a job with a big international company teaching Spanish to their employees—a slot that's vaguely in his field, but one that he hardly needed a world-class doctorate and loans up to his eyeballs to fill.) Maybe I just wasn't committed enough in my Francophilic ardor, but the prospect of ending up teaching bored, pimply adolescents the subjunctive mood sent me running in another direction fast.

Maybe you're an auto mechanic who's always dreamed of fixing planes. It's a terrific goal, but before jumping headfirst into this or any new field (and certainly before leaving your present job), do some research:

1. What kind of training will I need?
2. Where can I get it?

3. How much will it cost?

4. Are there jobs in the field?

5. Where are they?

6. What's the long-term prognosis?

Take a good, long look at these questions before deciding to make the move. I'm the last person to try to thwart your plans or squelch your enthusiasm, but make any move with your eyes and ears open.

Where to find all this out:

1. Your high school or college counselors.

2. Your city's office of career development.

3. Your own reading and research. (All medium-to-large cities have business libraries or substantial business reference sections in main library branches. The reference librarians are often excellent resources here.)

Is this easy? In all honesty, no. Most cities in today's America are severely underfunded, and their career resource centers are virtual jokes. Similarly, libraries aren't the same places those of us over thirty remember: With ever-decreasing funding and shortened staff hours, you may have to go to a big city's business library or an affluent suburban branch to find out what you need.

By the same token, schools' career/placement offices vary wildly in quality and scope. Columbia, from which I graduated in 1978, had a "placement office" whose motto might as well have been "Let them eat cake." Since the vast majority of my classmates went immediately to professional school, we hapless French, history, and philosophy majors were left to fend for ourselves. (I have a friend who went into the executive training program of a New York department store only because they were one of the few companies who came to interview undergraduates that year!)

On the other hand, Penn, where I went to graduate school, had a strong placement service about which even liberal arts graduates raved. The director of this office was plugged in to the full range of corporate and not-for-profit organizational life in Philadelphia and points beyond; it was, by all accounts, a smashing success. Drexel University, another Philly school known for its five-year work-study program and strong technical and business programs, offered top-notch placement for its students and grads.

If your school or city has a strong placement program, count yourself very lucky indeed. Because in today's world of downsized government and underfunded public institutions (here, I include libraries and state colleges both), the onus will fall more and more on you as to exploring job options and carving out your niche. This requires major work, to be sure, and it's something nobody ever told you you'd have to do as an adult, but your efforts have only one beneficiary: you.

• • •

Now, then. You've done your homework (an ongoing process, by the way) and are ready to start pitching in a new field. Unlike other career counselors, I am not asking you to list all your good or favorite qualities and compare them to the job you're targeting now. Deducing that your target is a reasonable one can only come from a comprehensive review of your target position(s), and their viability as targets given your present set of qualifications, education, and talents. If you are an auto mechanic, working on planes is a laudable goal, but you'll certainly need further training and certification before finding a job. By the same token, your German might be native-perfect and you may hold an advanced degree, but in many states you need certain teaching credentials as well. (Happily, the trend in education appears to be away from hiring people with the rather dubious "education major" and toward hiring people with intense knowledge of the subjects they're to teach—as has been the rule in Europe for centuries.)

Give me one more paragraph on my soapbox before I continue, and let me say this: Words can barely express my anguish at the lack of preparedness young people have about the range of careers available to them and the skills and education required to succeed in their careers. This phenomenon becomes increasingly disheartening as one travels down the socioeconomic scale. The other day on the news, for example, local TV crews were extolling the virtues of inner-city youth who stayed in high school and graduated on time (less than 30 percent in Los Angeles) instead of becoming pregnant, joining a gang, dropping out, etc. The Barbie-doll interviewer gushed incessantly about how marvelous these students were and how fabulously they would succeed. Just two weeks later, the *LA Times* ran a major feature on how even the top tier of these graduates lacked the test scores and college prep coursework required to get into the University of California system (much less an elite private college). Many of these students expressed the desire to become lawyers and doctors; unfortunately, their inadequate secondary school training makes this almost an impossible dream.

My point here is this: While I realize "big government" is

severely out of fashion, it will take a fully funded national program to educate young people—beginning in the early grades—as to preparation required for careers. It will then take concerted federal funding to bring not only urban schools but the average American school up to the level of other industrialized countries if we are to compete in the century to come.

Surprisingly, ignorance as to what people actually do isn't confined to the underprivileged; a large number of otherwise excellent candidates I've interviewed during my business career come to the meeting with the barest clue of what the company and/or my specific division does.

You, however, will know exactly what your target company does for one reason above all others: So you can tell them what you can do for them. And, sheer bravado aside, there's just no way that's possible without a strong knowledge of their daily business regimen. This is true even for like-like job hunts, and it couldn't be more true for people looking to segue into new fields.

So let's look at a case history of how one of my clients carved a new path by finding her own Perfect Pitch.

Jodie: From Publicity to Publishing

When I met Jodie through a mutual friend, I was immediately struck by how smart, charming, attractive, and yet terribly unsure of herself she was. She was working as a public relations manager for a sexy organization representing a major European country's food, wine, and related industries in the American market . . . a job that for many people would be a plum assignment, but which was driving Jodie mad.

As a career counselor, my first order of business is always

the same: in simple, nonerudite terms, to find out just what's going on. Believe it or not, this is easier than it sounds, and great fun for me: It's ever so rewarding to turn people on to new directions, to make that "Eureka!" lightbulb go off in their heads. It's human nature, isn't it, to be able to see someone else's life—professional as well as personal—more clearly than our own.

Sometimes, my clients have obviously done their own self-analysis and have very clear visions of where they want to go. Much of the time, they're realistic options, and I can start immediately to counsel them on achieving their goals; other times, their aims are pie-in-the-sky fantasies that I have to bring back down to earth.

First, I let Jodie talk. After a few minutes of pleasantries about our shared friend, our mutual love of anything French, and the atomic size of New York apartments (the last two of which I craftily made a mental note of!) I asked, "So tell me, Jodie, why are you here? What's going on at work?"

"Well . . . first of all, I have to tell you I feel a little strange even being here at all. My friends think I have a fabulous job and think I'm crazy for wanting to do something else."

"I know exactly what you mean. I've had glamour jobs I walked out on for a variety of reasons, and my friends thought I was stark raving mad. It's very easy to see a gorgeous office, prestigious company name, and beautiful business cards and think that's the end-all and be-all. But the most important thing to realize, Jodie, is that it's your life, and you have to do what makes *you* happy—not your friends."

"Agreed. It's just that I'm not sure what makes me happy at work."

"We'll find that out. And guess what: The job we get for

you may not be 'the one' or even your ultimate goal. But it will be one more step on the road to finding what makes Jodie really happy. In any case, it will be better than the job you have now, which obviously is causing you enough unhappiness to come see me."

"It's my boss that's causing my unhappiness. She's a fucking shrew."

(Laughing) "Now tell me how you really feel! I'm not discounting the very real possibility that the woman you work for is the dragon lady of all time, but there may be more to your current job problems than that. Let's begin at the beginning; tell me about your job."

"Well, I'm the public relations manager for a consortium representing the food and wine products of Country X. In the most general terms, my job is to publicize these products in the American marketplace, however that can be accomplished. It's rather more complicated than many straight publicity jobs, really, because the range of promotional options is huge. It's not just sending out press releases, which is what some run-of-the-mill publicists do. It's pitching story ideas to editors; arranging special events with restaurants and hotels, some of which are quite complex; traveling to Europe to meet with the companies we represent; doing special promotions with chefs; writing our company newsletter . . . well, there's more to it than that, but that's just the start."

"Actually, it sounds like a pretty great job. When I worked in the corporate world, most of my jobs had me bored silly, but this one sounds like there are lots of different functions and an unlimited range to make your imprint. I don't know about you, but I love juggling a lot of balls in the air at once!"

"Well, I hate it," Jodie nearly spat out. "I'm always trying to write, and people come in my office with piddly requests, and I have to manage outside people who can't do their jobs, and then my boss comes in with her unrealistic requests for more press for clients, most of whom I think are her personal friends—"

"Whoa, hold on just a minute, Jodie. To my mind, at least, the number one responsibility of a publicity manager is to get press. So in almost any company or agency you'd work for, your boss would periodically be down your neck at getting the company's clients more press. That's normal."

"Yeah, but I hate sucking up to the press. I mean, I love writing press releases and generating story ideas—if you ask me, that's what I do best—but I absolutely detest pitching stories and calling them back all the time. I feel like a used-car salesperson. That's not my personality at all."

"Well, then, I think we've arrived at our first unassailable truth. You shouldn't be a publicist."

"But I like some of the functions, such as arranging special events. I just hate hounding the press."

"Then maybe you could pursue work as a special events person somewhere, though I think that would make short shrift of your excellent education [Jodie was a liberal arts graduate of a great school] and writing skills. The point is, Jodie— and I reiterate—that the chief role of a publicist is to publicize. So if that's really anathema to you, you should certainly be doing something else."

"But what?"

"That's what we're here to figure out. You mentioned that you liked the writing aspect of your job. Talk to me about that."

"I've always loved to write. I was editor of my high school newspaper, and in college wrote for the literary magazine. In fact, I've published a couple of articles in food magazines, which was what helped get me this job," Jodie noted, her face lighting up for the first time since we met.

"Did you ever try to pursue a career as a writer?" I asked.

"I'd love to, but I thought it was unrealistic . . . that I needed a 'day' job."

"That you may, but you'll never be a writer unless you write. And speaking of day jobs, there are some in which you can write all day long. Ever heard of copywriters?"

"Of course," Jodie laughed, "but, frankly, the idea bores me. You're just dealing with someone else's ideas and expanding on them. And copywriters aren't very social creatures. Nobody ever takes them to lunch."

"Okay, Jodie. You want to generate your own ideas and have people take you to lunch. Your passion is gourmet food and beverage; you're a gastronome. You should be a food editor at a magazine or edit food books at a publishing house. That's what would have you smiling all day long."

"I'd love to do that," Jodie enthused, "but I never dared say that because I thought I'd never have a chance!"

"Never have a chance? But Jodie: you're a published writer, an authority on food and wine, have a fine degree, speak three languages, have a great job to put on your résumé, and are full of ideas in the field. What publisher wouldn't want you?"

"But, David, I've never been an editor. I'm just a publicist."

"Jodie, my love, no one is ever 'just' anything unless they choose to think of themselves that way. You can be anything you want if you have the determination to seek the training and skills required for a job. But in your case, you don't have to do anything but pitch yourself as an editor. You've got everything you need now."

"Well, it's nice of you to say so." Jodie blushed. "But magazines want experienced editors. I've never been one!"

"So you think God chooses people at birth and puts a sticker saying 'editor' or 'baseball player' or 'customer service rep' on their backs? He gives us certain dispositions and talents, but it's up to us to make the most of these. No editor in New York, the U.S., or the world was deposited behind a desk at birth."

"I guess, but . . ." Jodie trailed off, looking at the floor.

Clients like Jodie can be frustrating indeed. "What you need, young lady, is a little belief in yourself. I see tons of people in the work world who don't have a fraction of your gifts, who have vice president printed on their business cards. All it takes is a little chutzpah and belief in yourself."

"Okay, I'll try," Jodie offered.

"Say it with a little enthusiasm, please."

"I'll do it!" she said with conviction.

"Good," I replied. "Let's get started. Actually, though, our time is just about up. So this is your assignment for next week. Research the following: (1) food magazines, (2) lifestyle and travel magazines, (3) other magazines with food sections or columns, (4) newspapers with food sections, (5) food and liquor industry trade magazines, (6) publishing houses who do food or cooking books."

"That's a lot of work! How can I do all that in a week?" Jodie asked.

"You'll do as much as you can. The longer you wait, the longer you'll be unhappy where you are."

"But how do I find all this information?"

"Jodie, think for a minute. You're a big girl. With the exception of the publishing companies, you're pitching to these people—the magazines and newspapers—all the time!"

"But how do I find the publishers?"

"Now you're being a baby. You'll ask. You'll do some research. I could tell you where to go, but finding this information yourself will help you more—you'll be more involved in your job search. And quite frankly, since as a publicist you have the names of most of the people you'll be contacting on computer file, you have less work than ninety-five percent of my clients do from the get-go. Now, skedaddle. See you next week."

• • •

When Jodie returned the next week, she seemed more hopeful than I'd remembered her. "I can hardly believe how many names I have, how many publications in my industry exist! Maybe there's a chance there'll be an opening at one of them for me."

"Correction, Jodie. I'm delighted by your optimism, but you're still thinking in a passive mode. Instead, think about how many of these publications will be wowed by the range of qualifications you present to them . . . and how lucky they'll be to get someone who has worked at such a prestigious organization in your field."

"Do you really think so?"

"I know so; you just have to let them know what you can do for them. So let's begin. What are the major functions of a magazine or newspaper food editor?"

"She has to think up stories, identify new sources and trends, assign articles, edit them, work with photographers—"

"And what qualities would a *great* editor have?"

"All of the above, plus a special feeling for her subject . . . a vision, I guess you could say—like Diana Vreeland had at *Vogue* or Tina Brown had at *Vanity Fair.*"

"Good. That's exactly what you have to tell the editors-in-chief of the publications you want to work for."

"And book editors?"

"That's a separate, but far from unrelated pitch. We'll get to that next. Let's start with your primary target first."

I asked Jodie to draft a sample letter to prospect employers—in this case, editors. This is what she returned to me:

June 18, 1997

Ms. Barbara Pressman
Editor-in-Chief
GOURMAND MAGAZINE
345 Park Avenue
New York, NY 10017

Dear Ms. Pressman (or Barbara, in a less-than-superformal industry):

I am writing to inquire about editorial opportunities with *Gourmand* magazine, which I have read and admired for many years.

Currently, I am public relations manager for a company representing major European wine and food distributors. Thus, I know the gourmet industry inside and out.

I have also served as a freelance writer for several newspapers and magazines, with special emphasis on wines from Italy and France—a skill that would serve me well at

Gourmand. I hold a BA from Amherst College, and studied cooking at the American Academy of Gastronomic Arts.

I look forward to hearing from you. Thank you.

Sincerely,

Jodie Jones

As job letters go, Jodie's isn't terrible; there's nothing tragic about it, and a perceptive editor might see enough in her background to call her in.

Of course, by this point, you're already a studied enough disciple of the Perfect Pitch to know what Jodie's done wrong. Let's go through the exercise once more (even though I bet you really don't have to):

1. Jodie opened with the tired "writing to inquire about employment possibilities" phrase we Perfect Pitchers abjure. Instead, she should have opened with a unique proposition that sets her apart from paragraph one—a person who, whether or not a job opening exists, presents herself as an interesting person whom any editor would want to meet. (As I said before, in crafting your opening pitch, always keep this mission in mind: "Go on . . . I dare you not to see me!")

2. Jodie, like most people, overdoes the "I" thing. "Enough about yourself already; what can you do for me?" is the question the pitchee will be asking, and the one you should make sure to answer in every written or in-person pitch.

3. Jodie hasn't taken the time to lay out the transition from publicist to editor in terms that are not only obvious, but make her such a valuable commodity that editors will be saying, "Why didn't I think of that?" Nothing should be left to the pitchee's imagination; when you're attempting to change careers, even if it's not a 180-degree turn, you must do your best to assuage any possible objections and make your pitch proposition a no-brainer for the audience you're trying to convince.

4. I'll repeat it one more time: if you're sending out a mass mailing, you neither can nor should call all of the people to whom you've written. But with a highly targeted mailing like this, where you're writing to people in your field or an allied one, don't let the ball out of your court. Take an active role: Instead of the passive, almost cowering, "I look forward to hearing from you," close with "I'll call soon to set up a meeting convenient to you," "May we meet soon? I'll call to see what your schedule is like," or, if the person is a real bigwig, "I'll call your secretary [better still, show you've done your research by saying "I'll call Rosemary or Bill"] to see if I can get on your calendar next week."

Remember, when you call to schedule an appointment, be upbeat (yet never chirpy—don't mimic Kathie Lee Gifford or Richard Simmons here) and confident in who you are. Chances are, in our automated, understaffed age, you'll be speaking to voice mail and not a real, live human being. One approach I like:

"Hello, Barbara? Jodie Jones here. I hope you've had the chance to look at my letter, and that we can set up a meeting in the coming week. Please call me at (number) when you can; I look forward to seeing you soon. Good-bye, Barbara, and thanks."

I worked with Jodie to probe further, and make *her* tell *me* what elements of her background and experience would be of most interest to an editor. (I could have told her, but then she would have lost the hands-on practice of formulating a pitch. And, while my own knowledge of many industries is certainly broad enough to devise pitches for most of my clients, it's requisite that I go through the process with them if they work in highly technical or arcane fields.)

Having done this, we developed the following pitch:

June 14, 1996

Ms. Barbara Pressman
Editor-in-Chief
GOURMAND MAGAZINE
345 Park Avenue
New York, NY 10017

Dear Barbara:

How many food story ideas have I created in my thirty years on this planet? Scores . . . but here are my favorites:

- BRAVE BEYOND BRIE: an article on little-known French cheeses that appeared in the May 1993 issue of *Gourmand*.

- PRIMO PASTA: an exploration of make-it-at-home *paste* and regional sauces for hearty winter appetites.

- THE BEST OF EVERYTHING: a look at wines that are perfect with any meal, every day—in every budget range.

As head of publicity for a major consortium of European food and wine, I know the marketplace like no one else—and have a proven track record of pitching stories that have been placed in over fifty national newspapers and magazines.

Happily, I'm also a writer, and have contributed on gourmet topics to the *New York Times, Food Fiesta* Magazine, and—yes!—*Gourmand.* Thus, I'm not only a creative story person, but a seasoned writer/editor as well.

It goes without saying that I have vast contacts in the food industry, another trait that would help me create wonderful articles for *Gourmand* from day one.

Even if an opportunity doesn't exist right now, I'd love to meet to find out the magazine's future plans, and to discuss my background with you. I'll call soon to set up a meeting that's good for you.

Best and thanks,

Jodie Jones

By pitching to her audience's needs—by telling Barbara Pressman exactly what she can do for her and the magazine—Jodie has instantly transformed herself into a contender in the field, not just a public relations manager, but an insider of sorts.

This brings up a key issue: If there's an element necessary to your career transition, wishing and hoping that someone will want you despite your lack of qualifications is not going to make it. In Jodie's case, her published writings are a definite plus. Let's look at another example: If you're a secretary who wants to work in the finance division but lacks certain computer language skills, you'll probably be passed over for a job transfer; unless you work for a truly caring and progressive company, you'll probably see someone else hired, maybe even from outside the firm. Do all good things come to he or she who waits? Not in the job market. You're the only one who can make things happen, and if that means augmenting or updating your bank of skills, then you go, girl/boy—the power of your job future is in your own hands.

14
. . .

The College Pitch

"Yo Andrusia!" I hear you say. "I'm taking five classes, have two part-time jobs, and have about two hours per week of time to myself. You want me to start pitching, too?"

Unless you're in a sought-after undergraduate major like nursing or engineering, are in a top professional graduate program, or have a relative who's a U.S. senator or corporate bigwig, you're damn straight I do. You may think this is more work than you can handle, but trust me—a little far-sighted pitching now, and you'll be thanking me the day after you turn in that cap and gown. Try about three months of hearing "Come back when you have some experience" and you'll know exactly what I mean.

The perfect antidote: If you're still in school, *get* some experience. In most cases, it's easier than you think.

The key word here is *internship*. If you have even the vaguest notion of what you think your career should be, a soupçon of focused pitching can yield an internship, which serves two hugely important functions:

1. It will help you decide if that field is for you. (How many medical students run screaming the first time they see surgery being performed?)

2. It'll give you something wonderful to put on your résumé—that little extra that most graduating seniors
   won't have, and which can help you get your foot in
   your chosen door big time.

How do you get an internship? Your choices are obviously
far greater if you're going to school in or near a major metropolitan area, where the range of organizations in all sectors is vast. If
your college is in a rural setting, you'll have to reserve summer
vacations for catch-up time. In either case, this is what to do:

1. *Visit the career placement office of your school.* As I mentioned
earlier, these range from the ridiculous to the sublime. If yours
is in the latter category, you're in luck. Schedule a meeting with
the person in charge (some colleges will even have internship
directors), let him or her know what you're interested in, then
see what's available. Some especially conscientious career center
staffers will even take the lead, contacting organizations in your
field of interest if they're unaware of any opportunities when
you meet.

2. *Contact organizations directly.* Many companies and not-
for-profit organizations have established internship programs,
which make things 300 percent easier for you. After identifying
those for which you'd like to work (use the information in previous chapters as a guide), call the human resources or personnel department and ask for the lowdown, then follow through.

If the organization(s) you've targeted don't have a stratified
internship program, don't fear: Here's where you may really be
in luck. If you're able to talk to a personnel staffer who seems
willing to help you, milk them for all they're worth; find out
whom you should write to learn more. (In some cases, they
may volunteer to pass your note along. If so, don't try to cir-

cumvent them, but do follow up to make sure they're not just giving you the brush-off.)

Tell the personnel department person you're speaking to what you're studying, what your career goals are, and ask their kindness in recommending the head of that department so you can pitch him or her. For preprofessional majors (accounting, public relations, marketing, finance, engineering, etc.), this is a breeze. For English or philosophy majors, the onus is on you to do some research and discover where in an organization your talents might be used. (Your college career counselor should be able to impart good advice here.)

One example of a strong internship pitch:

Mr. Brad Bannister
Vice President, Accounting
Chainsaw Corporation
333 Industrial Way
Boise, ID 88888

Dear Mr. Bannister:

Could you use an able-bodied, highly disciplined University of Idaho student to serve as an intern several hours a week?

A junior accounting major with a 3.8 GPA, I'm seeking to supplement my academic coursework with hands-on experience. Given Chainsaw's excellent reputation, I can think of no place I'd rather do so.

What I can offer: sincerity, a can-do attitude, and a work ethic that's very strong. My résumé is enclosed to tell you more.

I'll call this week to see if we can schedule a short meeting to discuss this further. In the meantime, Mr. Bannister, thanks for thinking of me.

Sincerely,

Craig Craft

Suppose Bannister's secretary calls you, or you're able to get him on the phone, but you're told no internship program is currently in place. "That's fine," you'll tell him or her, "this isn't for academic credit per se. I'd just like to help you out for one afternoon a week to get some firsthand experience of accounting. I think it would prove beneficial for both of us."

I can only speak for myself, but I've never refused to see an enterprising student. Some states, by the way, have laws that restrict internships, but most don't; and, in any case, a little ingenuity can go a long way in allowing a nice young person to get some experience. I always put myself out because I'd hope someone would do the same for me.

After you've met with a representative of the target company, the universal pitching rule applies: Write a thank-you note. To the fullest extent possible this shouldn't be just an example of your marvelous grasp of etiquette, but a real opportunity to show what you know (or have learned) about the organization or firm. To wit:

Mr. Brad Bannister
Vice President, Accounting
Chainsaw Corporation
333 Industrial Way
Boise, ID 88888

Dear Mr. Bannister:

Thanks so much for taking the time to see me this week. I thought Chainsaw Corp. would be a great place to intern before our meeting, and now I'm sure.

As a member of your internship program [or, "as the charter member of your internship program" if none exists], I could lend a hand to one and all while learning the ropes. I think you know that I'm a workhorse, and one for whom no job is too big or too small. Given my willingness to contribute while viewing an account department's day-to-day activities, I believe a five-hour-a-week internship could benefit us both.

I'll call soon to follow up with you. In the meantime, Mr. Bannister, thanks for giving me the proverbial foot in the door.

Yours sincerely,

Craig Craft

By the way, if you're reading this and thinking, "Yeah, but every student from every college everywhere is trying to get an internship with this firm. I don't stand a chance": You're wrong, my friends. As in all things pitchworthy, most people just don't take that extra step. If you do, you're just steps away from the internship of your dreams.

"But I need a job that pays," you contend. "I can't give it away for free, even if it would look great on my résumé."

Understood; it's a valid point. So here's what you do: Work one afternoon a week one school year or one summer. I, too, had to put myself through school, and can empathize entirely with your point of view. Whether you interned a few hours a week or two days for four years doesn't make much difference; the important thing to a prospective employer is that you had the initiative to gain some experience in your field. (And some companies' internship programs actually do pay students who work there; it's a question of local laws and the organization's own policies.)

This brings us to another crucial point. When you're interning, do whatever your supervisor asks, unless it's illegal, immoral, or physically harms you in some way. Companies, you should know, have different rules: Some mandate that college interns do only "think work" and observation; at other firms, everything and anything goes. Whatever the policy, do what's asked, and do it with a kind heart and good cheer. After all, think how great the entry "Accounting Assistant" or "Public Relations Aide"—"titles" most people will kindly allow—will look on your résumé!

The prima donna routine will get you nowhere, and it's just as well you learned that now. Recently, my friend Ellie, who's head of International Publicity for a glamorous hair-care company, had an intern who turned up her nose at practically everything she was asked to do. Ellie took me to lunch and solicited my advice, which flowed freely: "Don't do this girl any favors; get rid of her—fast. Yours is one of the sexiest firms in New York, and there are literally hundreds of English and business majors in the City who'd give their right arm for a gig like that."

And so should you (well, figuratively at least!). An internship can mean the difference between a "nothing" first job and one that puts you well on your way to your ultimate career goals.

One other college-related pitch point that's a potential pitching pearl deserves mention here, and that's your college's (and/or graduate school's) alumni/ae magazine. If you're still in school, get a copy from the alumni office before you graduate, and comb it thoroughly to find people in your field. (You should use this as a potent tool throughout your career.) Alumni and alumnae of your school are a thousandfold more likely to meet with you, especially if you're gathering information, than someone who has no other connection with you.

Many colleges and universities also issue periodic annual alumni/ae directories listing all living graduates of the school. While these can be massive, the good news is that they are often categorized by profession, which makes them a virtual treasure trove of pitch targets. (My college directory, which comes out only every ten years—like Halley's Comet!—is scheduled to appear very soon, and I can hardly wait to get my mitts on one.)

15
· · ·

Networking: The Perfect Pitcher's Lifetime Tool

Ah, networking: the most misunderstood, misused, and—often —maligned arm in a job seeker's arsenal. (Also, all too often, the scariest.)

When I think of networking, two very different images come to mind:

1. The yuppie networking revivals ex-yippie Jerry Rubin used to hold at Manhattan's mammoth Palladium Club in the mid-eighties: crowded, crass gatherings of horny singles dreaming they'd find the mate and/or job of their dreams.

2. Marilyn Monroe in her showstopping number from *Gentlemen Prefer Blondes,* showering admirers with her famous half-open-mouthed smile and clutching a glass of champagne.

The first image, one of networking desperadoes, is at odds with the second, whose theme is networker-as-star. The truth, of course, lies somewhere in between.

What networking is: an ongoing process that all the most successful people use on a daily, yearly, lifetime basis—whether they're employed full time or looking for on-staff or consulting work. More than a finite activity, networking is more like a mind-set that ace pitchers use on and off the job to further their careers.

What networking isn't: a job-searching tool that stands on its own. Remember when your eighth-grade English teacher told you about the subjunctive case being not a tense, but a mood? The analogy applies perfectly to networking, which is more a frame of mind—a modus operandi, if you will—than an end result.

The reason I make these distinctions is simple: Many career counselors extol the virtues of networking as some sort of holy grail, a latter-day magic carpet ride that will fly you directly to the job of your dreams. Don't get me wrong. Networking is absolutely key, but it's part of a process, not the thing itself.

One career coach I know advises her disciples to use networking principles to see as many as seven potential employers in a week. In your dreams! To my mind, this kind of overly optimistic advice stalls job campaigns fast, as nobody—not even a Harvard MBA who looks like Naomi Campbell—is going to find such stunning success, especially in today's corporate economy, where people are overworked to a greater degree than ever before.

Sure, networking is important—*very* important. But don't believe what you may have read or heard about the hidden job market, nobody getting jobs through conventional methods, etc. More specifically, networking:

1. Does not absolve you from busting your butt looking for jobs using traditional approaches. (Remember, network-

ing is a process, not a discrete activity; it must be used in conjunction with other job-search techniques.)

2. Does not replace your own research and informational quest.

This second point requires clarification. Other career gurus advise clients—in books and in person—to use networking as an information-gathering tool. To some extent, this is true; but it should not be construed as a replacement for your own efforts. One guide, in particular, sees networking through impossibly rose-colored glasses, as if it were a Lewis Carroll–like neverland where job hunters are embraced by lovely souls desirous of sharing their gifts and points of view.

In popular parlance: Don't even think about it! With the exception of some low-key nonprofit organizations or educational institutions, there are very few folks out there who are waiting to spend half an hour telling you all about what they do out of the goodness of their souls . . .

. . . unless, of course, you are prepared to tell them what *you* can do for *them*. That, we know, is the bottom line in every winning pitch, and it's no different here—even if the pitch is just to get in the front door.

Many job seekers make the mistake of requesting an "informational" interview—"even," as the clichéd letter goes, "if no opportunities currently exist." My clients do not; in fact, I abjure the use of the oh-so-tired phrase, "on an exploratory basis, of course." Nobody has time anymore just to shoot the breeze; and besides, since it's obvious you're looking for a job, why be disingenuous and look like a passive information-gatherer? When it comes to direct mail, there's only one way "networking" works, and that's when the pitchee is so convinced of your special skills and drive that he or she wants to meet—to network, if you like—with you.

That said, don't even think about sending a letter like this:

July 1, 1997

Mr. Roberto Dinero
VP, Marketing

Dear Mr. Dinero:

Congratulations on your new position!

Since you are most certainly staffing up, I thought I'd share my résumé with you. Although my background is in food marketing rather than cosmetics, there may well be some related skills in my background that could be of interest to you.

I've been interested in entering the exciting world of toy marketing, and am especially keen on knowing more about your firm. Could we meet—on a purely exploratory basis, of course—to see where my background might help you out?

Kind thanks.

Sincerely,

Carl Clueless

This letter is, sadly, all too typical. Carl may have an excellent background, but as a pitchmeister, he's got a lot to learn.

His goal, obviously, is to get in to see Roberto Dinero in some vague hope of networking his way to a fab job in the toy biz. But Roberto's certainly too busy to do any hand-holding, and why should he? Here, Carl is using what he wrongly perceives to be "networking" as an excuse to do what he should have done before writing: work.

Now, just for a second, throw all of the above out of the window, because there's one case—just one—where an ingenuous, less-than-superknowledgeable information-gathering pitch can actually work: When you're still in school. Nobody expects a high-school or college student to know everything about the working world, and so those of you in this category are forgiven a multitude of sins. Don't get me wrong: You'll shine much brighter if you include a general knowledge of the company or organization in your pitch or at the interview, but this is the one instance where it's not absolutely necessary.

I write this from personal experience, because I have never once turned down an intelligent, heartfelt request for information from a student. (Maybe that's because I've received so few; take this to heart if you're a student reading this. Most of your classmates will leave this stone unturned—it's just "too much work"—so consider this virgin pitching territory for you!)

None of this means that a student's request for an informational interview should be halfhearted or vapid, as the following beseechment surely is:

May 3, 1997

Mr. David Andrusia
SWATCH WATCH USA
New York, NY 11111

Dear Mr. Andrusia:

I am a junior at Baruch College majoring in business, with a specialization in marketing, and am currently writing to companies to find out more information about what they do.

As Swatch Watch is a highly visible and trendy company, I would like to find out more about your marketing efforts vis-à-vis my future career. Can we meet to achieve this goal?

I look forward to hearing from you. Thank you.

Sincerely,

Laura Lax

Because she's still in school, Laura is allowed some lee-way—but not this much. As a business major, she should have more of a clue than this as to what marketing is all about and what she wants to do. At the very least, she should have called for a financial report, visited stores selling Swatch Watches, and call the firm's publicity office for more information—not even before the interview, but before pitching for one!

A far better interview pitch letter is this:

May 3, 1997

Mr. David Andrusia
SWATCH WATCH USA
New York, NY 11111

Dear Mr. Andrusia:

A company that established the highest market share in its category after just three years? As a marketing major at Hunter, I want to know more!

Like practically every other young person in America, I'm crazy about Swatch Watches (in fact, I'm embarrassed to admit how many I own!). But it's no wonder: Your company's disruptive advertising, high-profile corporate sponsorships, and way cool in-store displays grab your target customer and never let go. (The new boutique at Macy's is just about the most visually appealing thing in the store!)

Could you share just a few minutes of your time to tell me more about Swatch from an insider's point of view? I realize you're very busy, but even fifteen minutes would provide me with the insight I need to refine my post-Hunter job search.

I'll call soon to see when you can spare the time. Till then, thank you for thinking of me.

Sincerely,

Walter Wise

Unlike Laura's letter, Walter's shows enthusiasm, personality, and the ability to do his homework outside of the classroom. Walter has employed tools normally associated with pitching pros thrice his age:

1. He has complimented his audience without being obsequious. (Note his mention of the company's market share and innovative promotional techniques.)

2. He takes an active stance by telling his audience that he'll be following up with a call. (Though I'd bet that won't always be necessary—I, for one, would pick up the phone and call so enterprising a student as soon as I got his note.)

As much of a softie as I am for students with enough gumption to explore career options before they get out of school, there's one thing I can't abide: poorly written pitch notes. Not everyone is a born writer, but I am dismayed and horrified at the ghastly English used by college students today. (Unfortunately, if you fall into this category, you're not alone; many seasoned professionals share this malady.) If you're unsure of your language prowess, have a friend or your school's counselor proofread your letter before it goes out.

"That's all well and good for the student population," I hear you say with a cluck. "But what about the rest of us? Can't we network, too?"

Of course, you can; I already said so before. What you *can't* do, however, is write and ask for information like a twenty-year-old. Network as a means of gathering leads on what's happening where, who's going where, and where your talents can best be used, but, except in the case of friends and former colleagues, don't use networking as a passive tool. (Remember, if you think of networking as a process, not an activity unto itself, you'll be on the right track.)

Whether you're employed, hunting, or looking for freelance work, here's how to use networking to benefit you:

1. *As with all aspects of your campaign, decide what it is that you want. Without a target, you're not networking; you're flailing.* I can't tell you how many times I've been contacted by people—grown adults—who say something like this:

> "Hello, David? This is Dan Dizzi. I was referred to you by
> Ellen Kroner, our mutual friend—I think you know her?
> Well, um, I was like her assistant at Columbia Tri-Star? So,
> anyway, I'm kind of thinking about looking for something in

video? And she said, like, maybe you know something in that area?"

In what area, baby? I'm thinking. Directing videos? Writing them? Starring in them? Marketing videos? Or sweeping the floor in a video store? (Dan should've referred to the Seven Steps to a Perfect Pitch before picking up the phone: What does he want? I doubt he knows, as he can't articulate his goal to me.)

By the way, I hereby command everyone under the age of thirty to abandon at once the maddening slacker speech fetish of ending every sentence with a question mark. It signals indecision, undirectedness, and vapidity. While I understand this neogrammatical rule's emanation from Valley Girl/MTV English, it is neither hip nor charming, and will get you nowhere in the business or academic world. (It will, however, get you a job at the video store, if that's your goal.) By the way, although I would consider it highly presumptuous to correct someone's regional accent or grammar in an interview I was conducting, as a career counselor, I have no compunction about pointing out this annoying inflection to well-educated young people. If you're guilty of this crime, listen to yourself, or ask your friends to point out when you do this. It's easily correctable, and is important to your sounding professional and not at sea.

A much better pitch networking call would sound like this:

"Hello, David. This is Dan Dizzi; I was Ellen Kroner's assistant at Columbia TriStar" (slight pause to effect recognition, but never *"Do you remember me?"* the most self-deprecating phrase in the English language).

"Yes, of course, Dan. How are you?"

"Fine, David, thanks. David, the reason for my call is this: I'm looking for a job in the video industry, and Ellen said you know the field like no one else."

"Well, that's very kind of her. . . ."

"Yes, well, Ellen's a very kind person—which is why she was nice enough to give me your name. She may have told you that I have a degree in broadcasting from Ithaca College with a minor in business, and my primary goal is an entry-level position in video marketing. Could I pick your brain just a bit as to how to proceed—either now, or later if this isn't a good time?"

You get the picture. By presenting a clear picture of what he wants to do, Dan positions himself as a serious candidate—a decidedly different portrait from the one whose unfocused view reflected a not terribly committed professional aim. Even before I started charging to do this, I would gladly give the friend of a friend—be he or she student or seasoned pro—career-changing advice if that person struck me as serious in the least. On the other hand, I never waste time with people grasping for straws.

2. *Go through your Rolodex or computer file and compile a list of friends and associates who can help you.* If you're already working in a given field, these can be culled from (but not limited to) the following:

(a) Friends

(b) Colleagues (past and present)

(c) Editors at trade magazines

(d) Vendors (outside companies and professionals whose

services you use: They, more than anyone, often know who's making job changes in your industry.

Each of these groups should be treated differently; even among a category of contacts, how you network with them will be based in large part on how strong a relationship you've been able to cultivate with them. (Another apropos adage from Mom: "It's not *what* you know, it's *whom* you know.") If you're chewing your nails, thinking, Boy, I really should've gone to more industry functions, you're right. If you're job hunting and your contacts aren't what they should be, use this window of nonopportunity (as it were) to swear you'll never be caught short again, that the next time you find yourself looking for full-time or freelance work, your Rolodex will be bursting at the seams.

You know, of course, the saying, "Be nice to people on your way up. You never know whom you'll meet on your way down." Human nature being what it is, people love to high-hat those who have treated them like shit, and to give a leg up to people who have been kind. (Sometimes I find it hard not to subscribe to the theory that "Nice guys finish last," but then I remember how loving people were to me when Fox swallowed the firm I was working for whole: I had freelance work and free lunches coming out the kazoo. Take the high road, folks, and the same fine fate will be yours!)

Specifically, here's how to network with each of these groups:

(a) *Friends* will be thinking of you all the time and wishing you well. They'll call you the moment they spot an ad or hear of an opportunity—from a personal contact or via a headhunter—that has your name written all over it.

(b) *Colleagues* who are employed and think well of you will be happy to let you know when they hear of a gig that needs to be filled. They're also the best bets for freelance and consulting work, but don't mention what you're looking for in passing and then forget about it. If you're really serious about making money as a freelance, follow up with a letter and—very important!—business card, so you look like a serious professional, not an unemployed person fishing around for any work.

(c) *Editors* at trade magazines—and, even better, advertising salespeople—are fonts of information on staffing changes in the industry they serve. See page 145 on how these editors should know exactly who you are, no matter what field you're in.

(d) *Vendors* are gold mines in two ways: (1) like all of the above, they have a bird's-eye view of executive shuffling (after all, maintaining an up-to-date file of organizational rosters is their stock in trade); and (2) savvy job seekers can sometimes wangle a job *with* vendors if they play their cards right. For instance:

- Monica G., a creative director, needed a job fast when she was fired from hers; I helped her pitch her vendors (packaging houses, color separators, etc.) for an account exec job, which she got as a result of her fabulous industry contacts. (It wasn't her dream job, but it kept a roof over her head till she found the one that was—and employment of any kind is better than developing a first-name-basis friendship with Home Shopping Club hosts.)

- Paul P., a marketing executive, learned of an opening at one of the promotions agencies he used, and landed a job as its second-in-command. (Unlike Monica, for whom a vendor-generated job was a stopgap measure, Paul fell in love with the agency side and remains there still.) "Out of crisis comes opportunity" is the operative attitude here!

Note: The postpitch rules and regulations that apply to any meeting or phone contact apply here. To wit:

1. Be sure to dash off a short thank-you note to anyone who's even moderately helpful. (I myself use funky post-cards to thank people in all but the most buttoned-down fields; people at work are usually tickled to receive any-thing not written on boring business stationery, and this helps to establish my own personality. Or, handwrite a note on good quality, traditional stationery you've or-dered at a paperie or stationery shop—never a Xerox joint, where something in the end product inevitably screams "cheap.")

2. Wherever possible, leave the phone call or meeting with the names of several other people who might be of use. You might, for instance, use this approach: "Phil, you've been very helpful, and I'm grateful for all the informa-tion you've been able to impart. Before I go, may I ask one more kindness: Do you have any colleagues who might be in need of my services?"

   If Phil seems ready to conjure up a batch of names, get your pen and paper ready. If he seems momentarily stumped, I usually add, "Oh, you don't have to tell me now. What if I called you next week [or "on Friday," if it's still early in the workweek] to pick your brain?

Would that be all right?" Experience has shown that all but the biggest ogres are happy to refer you to other people in their company or colleagues elsewhere whom you should target.

Know, of course, that this approach works wonders if you're: (a) sourcing freelance/consulting work, or (b) conducting informational interviews. If you're meeting someone to talk about a specific job, asking for referrals during the interview process would be highly inappropriate (if not downright gauche!).

But what if you've had one or more "good" meetings with an organization, but ultimately didn't get the job? Should you slink away with your tail between your legs and croon an especially depressing version of "Maybe Next Time"? No, *mes chers;* this is the time to milk that sympathy vote for all it's worth. (If, that is, there was good-to-excellent chemistry between you and the person(s) you met; the horror-story meetings we've all had our share of wouldn't warrant this approach.)

You've already seen how one job seeker used what I call the "first runner-up" letter to his advantage (page 117). Let's take one more look at how the Perfect Pitcher squeezes every possible opportunity dry:

Ms. Anna Swenson
President
Travel Options, Inc.
111 Main Street
Honolulu, HI 99999

Dear Anna:

Meeting you last week to discuss the position of travel consultant was a great pleasure indeed.

While I'm disappointed that you've decided in favor of another candidate with more cruise industry experience, I do hope you'll consider me for the next opening with your firm. (In the meantime, I am taking your advice, and have already signed up for a seminar on cruising to be offered by the American Society of Travel Agents next month.)

Anna, I'm writing to ask if you might know of any other opportunities in the travel field, either in Honolulu or elsewhere on our gorgeous islands. While I'm certainly pursuing ads and writing to Hawaii's better agencies, word of mouth is important in researching jobs, so I'd be grateful if you'd let me know of anything you might have heard.

I'll call early next week to see if you have any tips to share. In the meantime, Anna, meeting you was great fun, and I do hope we have the chance to work together soon.

Best and thanks,

Jean Simonelli

Ninety-nine percent of job hunters accept being the also-ran as some kind of consolation prize. Perfect Pitchers like Jean know that the real bounty may only later be revealed; ergo, her follow-up letter to Anna Swenson, which serves three strong purposes:

1. A lovely thank-you positions you as a class act, no matter what field you're in. Plus, we've already seen how, when the final candidate doesn't work out or leaves a job, you can turn being number two or number three on the food chain into a position for you. (Remember that old salvo

from beauty contestants: "If, for any reason, the winner cannot fulfill the responsibilities accorded her by the title Miss Universe, the first runner-up will assume her duties." The same proviso holds true for job seekers as well.)

2. By alluding to her seminar attendance, Jean both compliments Anna by following her advice (note that adhering to constructive criticism is a sign of maturity and wisdom; apple-polishing is not!) and lets Anna know that she is expanding her knowledge of the travel field. (And isn't an employee big on self-improvement one we'd all love to have around?) The bottom line here: Instead of closing the door on the possibility of a future with this travel agency, Jean is keeping it open by furthering Anna's positive impression of her.

3. More immediately, Jean is using this as the perfect opportunity to network by uncovering any travel industry jobs Anna may know of. (And even if none strikes her immediately, Anna will certainly mention Jean's name first when a colleague mentions an opportunity to her.)

Note throughout all of the above example that Jean isn't networking to find out information on her industry, but rather to exert her influence within it. At the risk of overstatement, keep this networking axiom firmly in mind:

Ask not what a company can do for you;
ask what you can do for the company!

Whether you're a veteran in the field or someone trying to edge his or her way in, networking isn't for organizations to tell you about themselves. Rather, it's a way for you to tell them what you can do for them; in short, to exhibit your Perfect Pitch in every possible way.

There's one other aspect of networking that we haven't discussed, and it may well be the most important one of all: using the resources of trade associations to get ahead.

The first way you can use trade organizations—those governing bodies of officialdom that preside over every imaginable professional field—is to obtain their membership lists. Some charge, some don't, and some, for a price, will even provide you with pressure-sensitive stick-on labels that make direct mailing (for full-time work or freelance jobs) a breeze. The beauty here is that these names and addresses are generally far more accurate than in the relatively more disinterested directories you'll use; thus, calling to check for accuracy isn't as vital as it is when you're culling names from guides.

The second way to milk these organizations is to participate in everything they have to offer. You say you're not a "joiner"? Hell, neither am I; we Scorpios would rather hide under a rock and write about a meeting or get-together than actually be part of one. So trust me on this one: Even if you're the proverbial shrinking violet, it's far easier to mix (and maybe, match!) with people who share at least one point of commonality—your field of work—than with strangers in a bar. And you don't have to attend every workshop and bash; a select few are all you need to do to make your presence known.

The benefits here are self-evident:

1. People will know who you are.
2. You'll know who other people are, and what they do, making your next job hunt a relative piece of cake.

This, by the way, underscores a point I made earlier—namely, that blind networking isn't the miracle worker many career counselors crack it up to be, unless (sorry for stating this to the point of tedium) you're still in school. But when you're already hooked into colleagues in your field (even if tenuously), touching base with these people when you're job hunting is no longer networking blind. Do you see now what I meant by networking being a process, not a technique unto itself?

The third and least known way to milk marketing muscle from your industry's trade associations is to be in them. Now, calm down; I can hear some of you screaming from thousands of miles away. Nothing gets a rise out of my clients so much as this suggestion, and I understand why: The mere suggestion of toiling for a trade organization conjures up images of gray offices with depressing, Truman-era furniture and rotary-dial phones. Felt-tip pens? Expense accounts? "No way," I hear you say.

In distant times, the above vision may well have held true. Not anymore; today, most trade organizations know they have to be sexy to sell themselves both to member companies and the outside world, and the externals are a big part of that plan. Therefore, your first fear should be promptly allayed: Working in this area is no longer the professional equivalent of being a nun.

In fact, some of the glossiest, glitziest people I know have recently signed on to senior posts in their trade association with all the pluses and promises of a high-profile corporate job. (After all, what high roller would make the move from private industry without these perks?)

First and foremost, then, is that these jobs can be challenging and fun. Even more important, they can be sensational stepping-stones to a wonderful job in your chosen field. Think of it: What company wouldn't want to hire someone from a position of omniscience—someone who knew everything that was happening in its field? (This presupposes, of course, that you have the basic skills to succeed in your given area of expertise.)

My favorite illustration of this career path is a dynamic young woman I'll call Lynette, who was in every way a winner —until the California recession of the early-to-mid-nineties, during which time she lost an account supervisor position with one of the country's most talked about advertising firms, where she worked on a movie studio account. Despite sterling qualifications, Lynette—and many other top candidates—were virtually shut out of two industries (movies and advertising) where companies were consolidating and downsizing, and in which practically no one was adding staff.

Lynette wasn't the type to sit around and mope, however; so when a friend suggested she join a volunteer committee at a leading organization governing the motion picture industry, she jumped at the chance. Later, when she saw some of the other names on the benefit committee, her heart nearly skipped a beat: Several Oscar-winning directors and executives from nearly all the studios were on the list.

Did Lynette shrink to the background, cowering in some corner? Not in this lifetime, baby. She walked into the first meeting as if she owned the place. (Remember, though, what I said earlier about the difference between confidence and belligerence!) When the head of the committee took nominations for a co-head, Lynette nominated herself: "Madame Chairman," she proposed, "I've just wrapped up a major marketing assignment and think I can contribute the time this worthy benefit program deserves if it is to succeed." Need I tell you her self-nomination was confirmed in five seconds flat?

Lynette took charge immediately, working harder on this benefit than she had at any job. But did she spend these three months bugging influential board members for a job? Not at all; that would have resulted in a highly imperfect pitch. Instead, she took the bull by the horns, almost singlehandedly orchestrating a wildly successful gala—handling all the advertising and publicity, of course!—and showing her prominent colleagues just what she could do.

Did she milk these connections for all they were worth? She certainly would have—except that she didn't have to. Before she could say good-bye and thank her board members on the night of the fête, Lynette was slipped two business cards from studio bigwigs, and, two weeks later, she was named to a senior marketing post with one of the largest movie studios in the world.

Are results like this guaranteed? Of course not; nothing in life is a free ride. But I promise you this: Working for a trade organization or allied component thereof is a terrific way to segue into a private post in your field. Moreover, you don't have to be in a highly visible part of the organization like marketing or publicity to achieve this goal; whether you're a membership director, administrative assistant, or financial person, making the move to private industry is highly possible if you use the pitching techniques discussed throughout this book.

16
. . .

The Paper Pitch: Your Résumé

Six little letters—but, oh, the awe they inspire! One small word that's been known to make grown men and women tremble as they pore over every word, pout over poor print jobs, and pit ivory bond against off-white rag. And with good reason: job hunting is stressful, and the added distraction of trying to choose among paper stocks and font styles is enough to make anyone jump off the bridge. (Especially if you're as inherently indecisive as me!)

So once again I'm telling you to calm down, take a deep breath, and chant, mantra-like: "My résumé is my friend. My résumé is my friend." Do it until you believe it—and here's why you should:

1. *Unlike in days of yore, the résumé is no longer an immutable object, typeset with the definity of hieroglyphics on stone.* (When I got out of college, you had two options: typewriting your résumé, which always looked crummy, or paying a print shop to typeset it for you, which was so expensive you freaked out over any stray comma or change you might need to make.) So:

Don't make the preparation of your résumé a task to be dreaded; since you'll undoubtedly be writing it on a computer, you can make changes in a minute flat. This brings us to the next point.

2. *Consider your résumé flowing, changing, a near-gaseous element set to conform to your momentary desires.* As you will be altering it constantly as an arm in your arsenal of the Perfect Pitch, its molecular composition on any day is less important than how you use it. (Is that Zenlike, or what?)

3. *Use white or ivory (also known as buff, nude, off-white, and a variety of other "Color Me Beautiful"–type names!) bond of a good weight—period.* Pink, lavender, and robin's-egg blue are great for printing flyers advertising bake sales, but not résumés. Gray isn't businesslike, merely depressing; avoid it like the plague.

4. *Experiment with fonts; the best way to choose one is to find a résumé you think looks especially sharp, and ask its owner which typeface he or she used.* If you're looking for guidance, I can assure you that Times New Roman is always a superprofessional, highly readable choice. Always use 12-point type; 10-point is too small and thus hard to read.

5. *Think of your résumé as a forum for presenting your duties and achievements in each job you've held.* As long as you accomplish this goal clearly, concisely, and readably, you're one step ahead. Remember this: Your most important pitch will come from your cover letter and in-person pitch—the interview. The résumé is just a conduit, a means of getting you in the door, not a showpiece to be displayed in museums for time immemorial. Rembrandt undoubtedly obsessed about getting every brushstroke right; you needn't lose sleep over your résumé. Does it say what you've done, where, and why you were a star at each job? If so, then your résumé's fine.

6. *Based on my own experience as a hiring authority and on countless conversations with executive recruiters, please take the following directly to heart:*

(a) Always use a chronological résumé; that is, one that lists your jobs in sequential order. Functional résumés (or the utterly confusing and misdirected "combination résumés") signal the very thing they seek to avoid: changing careers, prison stints, or periods of unemployment. In this sense, they're like salt in the wound, rather than achieving their ostensible goal of smoke-and-mirroring your past. Ten years ago, changing jobs was career suicide; given the changing face of employment (and economics) in North America, it no longer is. Functional résumés are like pancake makeup: They just call attention to the problem, never eliminate it completely. If you have one gaping hole in your lifeline, say you were a missionary, a singer in Paris, or something else mysterious, exotic, or ultrahumane. But avoid the functional résumé—it's just one big mushy mess.

(b) Do not (as at least one major career book oddly advises) make your résumé a virtual storybook of your life and times. Do not include a picture of yourself, unless you're targeting the stage and screen or a gig with Heidi Fleiss. And if you remain committed to the idea of putting your mug on your résumé, *never* do so attired in some bizarre native garb or posed next to farm equipment. Please! (Similarly, your height, weight, and color of hair and eyes are only apropos if stripping is your chosen field.)

7. Do change your résumé like the change of the wind to reflect more fully the skills and background sought for a given job. You've already seen how to mold and form a pitch cover letter to respond to specific job ads; similar flourishes in your résumé can make the difference between being seen and being thrust into the "no" pile.

This point of view is corroborated by Carole Katz, director of executive recruitment at Warner Brothers, and one of the most respected human resources executives in the country. "Keep your résumé brief and to the point," she advises. "One page does it for most people, two for seasoned managers. People scan résumés for a few brief seconds, so it's important that key points be immediately recognizable and clear." And her attitude toward functional résumés can be summed up in one word: "No," she warns, "because they inevitably raise more questions than they answer, besides being convoluted and difficult to read."

In other words, use the format of the example provided here as a template. The person scanning your résumé should be able to pick out your job titles and the companies for which you've worked at the briskest glance. Since the huge numbers of résumés coming in for any given job are immense—especially in response to an ad—anything but a perfect fit is eliminated. This is also why you should, with the approval of your former boss(es), have the liberty of amending your job title in today's hypercompetitive times.

This is very easily accomplished and represents that little stroke that Perfect Pitchers use well. Let's say you're a nurse working in a doctor's office, but have decided you'd rather be in the fast-paced world of an ER. (In point of fact, most nurses have traditionally made the opposite move; today, given the sexiness of the hit TV show, I'm seeing a slight trend back to the war zone!) So let's say this nurse's most recent résumé entry looks like this:

Nurse/Manager   1993–1997
Office of Dr. George Gaines
Pensacola, FL

Managed front office and cared for patients for prominent internist.

- Oversaw all administrative details, including patient and insurance processing, supply ordering, and ap-pointment scheduling.
- Nursed patients as needs required, with special em-phasis on short-term emergency care.

This is fine; it tells what this nurse did, and positions her perfectly for another doctor's office job. But it doesn't target her for an emergency room post, which is what she's seeking now. Naturally, she will explain her burning desire to be on the front lines in the cover letter, but she will also rearrange her résumé to emphasize her daily dealings in emergency care. Thus, the entry would now look like this:

Nurse/Manager   1993–1997
Office of Dr. George Gaines
Pensacola, FL

Responded to all patient needs, from emergency to long-term care.

- Nursed emergency patients through all phases of care, working with doctor to provide immediate treatment, including preparation for in-office surgery, stitching, etc.

- Cared for patients during office visits, both routine and special.

It's clear that this nurse knows that in order to segue to the emergency room world, a pitch is not just a luxury, but an integral part of her job campaign. In the same vein, you should use the kindness of computers to change entries on your résumé to more perfectly suit a potential employer's needs.

8. A "Summary of Qualifications," "Summary of Experience" (or, more grandiosely, "Summary of Achievements") is fine, indeed helpful, if you have worked in several phases of a given field, and wish to show organizations the breadth of your professional range. Consider this résumé I wrote for a client just days ago:

MICHAEL BARSEVICH
340½ N. Stanhope Avenue
Los Angeles, CA 90036
(213) 921-0000

Summary of Qualifications

Nineteen years' successively responsible experience in all phases of the television industry, with special emphasis on live program production and writing/directing documentaries and on-air promotions. An Emmy- and Iris nominated producer/director and seasoned manager with top-drawer creative and organizational skills.

Professional Experience

DIRECT ADVANTAGE MARKETING   1995 to present
Operations Director

Chief operations executive for major fund-raising organization serving the broadcasting and other industries.

- Conceived and implemented direct marketing campaign raising over $1 million to benefit WQED (Pittsburgh Public Television) and WLIW (New York Public Television).

SENIOR DIRECTOR/PRODUCER   1993 to 1995
University of Pittsburgh Medical Center

Managed all phases of audio/video promotional programs for internationally recognized research and teaching medical center.

- Wrote and directed educational/medical videos.
- Developed materials for television and radio advertising campaign.

INDEPENDENT DIRECTOR/PRODUCER   1991 to 1993

Wrote, directed, and produced television programs and promotions for major clients in Pittsburgh area.

- Conceived and developed "Stop, Look & Cook," a nutritional program series for children.
- Produced and directed a United Way fund-raising video for the Westinghouse Corporation

PRODUCTION MANAGER   1991
WFLX-TV (Fox Network)

Managed production department for West Palm Beach, FL, affiliate of major television network.

- Directed all activities of commercial production department, supervising staff of five.
- Liaised with sales staff to formulate short- and long-term promotional plans.

DIRECTOR/PRODUCER   1981 to 1991
WTAE-TV (ABC)

Produced programs and on-air promotions for Pittsburgh ABC affiliate station.

- Emmy nomination for producing "Project Bundle-Up," which resulted in $2 million in donations to the Salvation Army.
- Winner, Best Pennsylvania TV Campaign (Director, "Joe Said It Would").
- Winner, AWRT Award for Best TV Talk Show ("Pittsburgh's Talking").

Education   1980

Southern Illinois University, B.S., Radio/Television

- Graduated summa cum laude with University Honors

My client had a wonderfully comprehensive background in the broadcasting field, but it was just this side of "all over the place." Moreover, Mike's most recent job was a semi–stopgap one that was highly tangential (at best!) to his career trajectory and goals. (It was, in fact, fueled by cutdowns in TV station staffs across the country; if you, too, have been affected by consolidations or cutbacks in your industry, you're not alone; and temporary sidetracks to keep a roof over your head no longer carry the stigma they once did.)

As you can see, we accentuated the positive, especially in Mike's last job as a fund–raising executive. Since he ideated and managed campaigns for two public television networks, we gave these clients prominence to foster the illusion of continued, direct involvement in the broadcasting game.

If you're one of those (increasingly few!) people who have maintained a steady career path in a given field, and want to continue the (increasingly rare!) "traditional trajectory," a summary of achievements is otiose. People in your area will know exactly where you've been and what you've done through the individual entries of your résumé; you're absolved from tying everything up in a neat little package because you *are* a neat little package.

9. *Including an "Objective" at the top of your résumé does nobody any favors.* This is true because: (a) if you're in a given field and want to continue, it's obvious what your objective is, and (b) if you're trying to make a career change, simply tacking "Objective" atop your CV is akin to waving a magic wand—only it won't work. If you're segueing into a new field, a pitch cover letter and rousing interview are the only ways to make this happen. Plopping an objective down on your résumé is nothing more, alas, than wishful thinking on your part.

10. *Finally, be sure your pitch letter and résumé are printed on exactly the same kind of paper.* If you only think they match or are "close enough," they aren't. (Fine bond paper is cheap enough at places like Staples and Office Depot that no one should be without a big, thick stack at all times, thus avoiding the momentary impulse of thinking mix 'n' match looks okay. It doesn't; case closed!)

The lion's share of résumés in career guides (and even specialized résumé preparation manuals) is devoted to individuals in the business world. The following is an example of a clear, insightful résumé for a mental health practitioner in San Francisco.

Note that, unlike business people, it is difficult for people in other fields to work their résumés into the preferred "responsibilities . . . achievements" format. A psychotherapist, for example, could hardly say (at least, without sounding ridiculously stilted and somewhat pretentious), "Fifty percent of patients left my practice after six months due to much-improved mental health." If you're in marketing, sales, or allied fields, it's easy to quantify achievements statistically; for other professional areas, it's less so. One interesting exception to this rule is that of teachers, who can include quantifiable results such as "Helped improve mathematics testing scores by 23 percent over previous year."

The final word: Don't listen to the guides that tell you to quantify your achievements, no matter what. It's just not possible in many fields. As I said before, as long as your résumé states clearly what and where you've done and outlines your achievements to the fullest extent possible, you're home free.

MICHAEL AHERN, MFCC
414 Gough Street
San Francisco, CA 94102
(415) 252-0226

EXPERIENCE

1990 to present   *Independent Psychotherapy Practice,*
San Francisco

Provide psychotherapy to individuals and couples in independent office practice.

1989 to present   *Staff Therapist,*
OPERATION RECOVERY

Supervise interns' group therapy practicum, applying knowledge of and training in models of group dynamics and leadership.

Assess clients, presenting problem, mental status, health status, social and medical support, awareness of and compliance with HIV transmission prevention, financial/employment status, and family history among other issues.

Formulate conceptualizations based on client assessment and make preliminary diagnoses along with treatment recommendations, to include alternate or adjunctive services in the community (residential treatment, detox, social, and medical services), as appropriate.

Provide counseling and psychotherapy to single-, dual-, and tri-diagnosed clients (HIV/substance abuse/mental disorder), with knowledge of a sensitivity to the psychosocial and medical issues they present, coordinating with other providers as needed. Make referrals, providing any necessary coordination, transitional support, and/or follow-up.

Participate in and contribute to case conference at which dispositions and consultations are made with a medical consultant, team manager, and peers.

1994 to present *Consulting Clinical Supervisor,* HAIGHT ASHBURY PSYCHOLOGICAL SERVICES

Supervise the work of interns at this outpatient clinic, with special emphasis on treatment of alcohol and drug abuse.

1988 to 1989   *Intern,* OPERATION CONCERN
Treated individuals and couples under
the supervision of a psychodynamically-
oriented psychologist, while receiving
extensive training in community mental
health.

1987 to 1991   *Substance Abuse Counselor,*
BAY AREA ADDICTION RESEARCH
AND TREATMENT

Learned and practiced principles of
cognitive-behavioral substance use treatment. Provided counseling to a diverse
client population (many residents of San
Francisco's Tenderloin district) in this de-
manding setting.

1986 to 1987   *Co-Facilitator,*
HENRY OHLHOFF HOUSE

Co-facilitator of group process in this
social-model substance-abuse treatment
program.

EDUCATION   M.S., 1990
San Francisco State University

B.A., 1978
Columbia University

LANGUAGES   Fluent in Spanish and French;
working knowledge of Italian.

17
· · ·

The In-Person Pitch:
Interview to Win!

When I was in graduate school, there was a woman who had the stuff of which legends are made. Hollie, as I'll call her, was hardly your average Wharton woman; instead, she was a brash New York hitter chick who'd graduated top of her class at the City University of New York and wended her way into Penn's hallowed halls of Ivy.

That fact alone should tell you: Hollie was a master of the pitch.

At graduation, when people were scrambling for jobs, Hollie was able to pick among six fabulous offers, all from high-profile, blue-chip packaged-goods firms. (That might not be your cup of tea, but for marketing MBAs, it's a time-honored golden stepping-stone to other jobs.) Needless to say, her more well toned classmates were jealous as hell.

Yes, Hollie was rather rough around the edges, with not quite the right suit and a Queens accent that could cut a knife. But Hollie had something no one else had: an innate sense of the pitch that transcended everything else; and she had major international companies begging for her employ.

Before she left campus, I begged Hollie for her secret. (We were the only two proto-punks on campus, and were thus intimates of sorts.) "Honey," she snorted, "ya gotta love them cans."

"Excuse me?" I asked, baffled.

"The *cans,* baby, the *cans.* As in Del Monte and Dole."

"So what's so important about the cans?"

"Sweetheart, you got a lot to learn," Hollie chuckled, proffering her trademark Marlboro Red. "The cans are the *product* —and every company wants to hear how fabulous their products are."

"So you told Dole and Del Monte you loved their cans?"

"No, dummy—I told them I worked in my Uncle Vito's grocery store in Flushing for three summers straight, and that's how I knew I wanted a career marketing packaged goods. I told them the only thing that kept me sane doing stock work was to read every label, make mental comparisons about the products, and do some street-level marketing of my own."

"Hollie, I can hardly see you stocking cans of peas."

"Well, kid, I did—for about five minutes one summer before Vito said I spent too much time talking to guys."

"So what about the three summers you told Del Monte about?"

"What they don't know won't hurt them. For that matter, I told them my uncle so valued my opinion he had me working on promotions and merchandising with food companies' sales reps."

"Oh, yeah, right. And you said this with a straight face?"

"A poker face. And they ate it all up. Listen, honey, you and I both know I can't compete with these Yale and Wellesley babes with their old families and thousand-dollar suits. So I had to create a persona that would do myself proud. And what better success story than the girl from Jackson Heights who made it to Wharton by stocking cans in her uncle's grocery store, where she fell in love with packaged goods?"

"Only Hollywood could create such a story. . . ."

"No, David—*I* created it. Get my drift?"

• • •

Of course I got Hollie's drift, and I thought it was brilliant. She knew damned well she couldn't compete with Muffy and Martha on their playing field so she created a new one all her own. And the little white lie about the three summers couldn't possibly hurt anyone. Which brings us to another . . .

Very Important Point: Elaborating on your background is perfectly acceptable—in fact, it's an integral part of a truly Perfect Pitch—as long as it doesn't hurt anyone or isn't an outright lie. For instance, you should never lie about your education, actual achievements (citations, honors, etc.), and other factual information; nor should you take credit for other people's accomplishments.

You can, however, embellish within reason, and you must trust your own instincts as to what this is. In Hollie's case, for instance, a visitor from Mars could spend fifteen minutes in a supermarket and make certain deductions about how items are stocked and shelved, what kind of promotions are in place, etc. (Plus, of course, she had actually studied this in detail in school.) Expanding on her rather short period of grocery employment was the only way she could compete with silverspoon types, and doing so harmed no one in any way. On the other hand, calling yourself a brain surgeon when you've never been to medical school is a ruse that (obviously) could bring grotesque and horrible results, and is thus not a highly advisable (or, certainly, likely!) "corrugated pitch."

I myself stretched the truth by telling Revlon that I was a part-time makeup artist. (Well, I was, kind of—when we went pogo-ing at New Wave dance palaces, I always painted everyone's faces, including my own.) Creating this revisionistic bit of personal history was in no way injurious to my job—I was marketing their products, not working with them, for God's sake—but added a touch of mystique that piqued interest in the person who hired me.

Similarly, I told New Line Home Video that I not only loved the art videos they distributed but was crazy about *City Slickers,* one of their big releases of the year. I cackled along with my new boss, who insisted on recounting some of the movie's tired bits ad nauseam, when I really felt like retching; but my feigned interest helped establish a sort of camaraderie, and I ultimately got the job. (In actuality, I hate Billy Crystal—he's like every moderately funny loudmouth at summer camp I always wanted to smack.)

The point, I think, is clear: It is beholden on you to express devout love and admiration for the company and its product or service as a vital component of your in-person pitch. You must do so, however, in a sincere and not obsequious manner, the difference between which should be immediately clear to you.

For instance, if you're interviewing as a customer sales rep at a clothing manufacturer, don't start shrieking, even before the interview has begun:

"Ohmigod, is that a Madonna Ferrin? I love her clothes, that's why I want to work here! My friend Shannon has the same top you're wearing, I was like so jealous, it cost one twenty-five, like I could afford it—of course, her boyfriend gave it to her, she's such a slut—but if I got a job here, I'd get a discount, right? I mean, don't employees get Madonna Ferrin clothes cheap? Oh, I went to

Universe Thirty-one, that discount clothing store downtown, it's supposed to be so cheap, like right, Saks even has better sales except they're usually out of my size by the time things are marked down 'cuz I'm the most popular size, an eight, but that's only because I go to the gym, otherwise I'd look like a house. As if I'd get a boyfriend like Shannon's, anyway, who could buy me MF clothes, they're just so fabulous. So, like, how are you?"

Sound contrived? I've conducted interviews where the over-zealous candidates were just as wired and fawning as this.
Nor should you play it disinterested and cool, à la:

Most people probably come here for the glamour of the fashion business—like Madonna Ferrin would even look at the underlings anyway. No, I'm here because to me, customer service is customer service, and if I'm on the phones handling people's problems, it doesn't matter whether I'm working for a fashion company or the sanitation department of New York."

A wiser, more intermediate approach, interjected at an opportune time during the interview might be:

"Well, I admit it: Clothes are my passion. In fact, I worked at clothing stores all through college to help pay my way. So, yes, the thought of working here is very appealing to me. But ultimately, what this job is about is customer service, and that's where I really shine. As you know, I spent two years as a customer service rep for a major credit card company—and, as you can imagine, if ever there were a great training ground, that was it. But I appreciated that experience, because I was able to learn just about every aspect of the customer service area, and think I did well—I was employee

of the month twice. I feel, though, that now is the perfect time to combine my expertise in the field with my love of fashion, so I can think of no better place to be than right here. Wouldn't you agree?"

In the above example, the candidate has done everything right. She has:

1. Spoken of her experience in the customer service field, mentioning her citation.
2. Alluded to her love of fashion (without being overpowering or obvious).
3. Shown she can make a clear, cogent, concise point.
4. Shown that she has examined exactly where she wants to be in her career.
5. Invited the interviewer to agree with her assessment—which, of course, is so well thought out that no one could possibly disagree!

You get the picture, don't you? When you interview, every twist, every turn of the conversation should be redirected back to your pitch. Whether the question is about last night's ball game ("Yeah, the Mets are cooking—I think it's because they're working better together as a team than they have in years. In fact, that's not unlike myself: I'm a great team player too, which is a quality I think would be most useful in this job. For instance, in my last position . . ."), the weather ("You got that right, Baton Rouge is sizzling today—kind of like your own Cracklin' Cajun Hot Sauce, wouldn't you say?"), or (as it sometimes happens) the job at hand, you should seize every opportunity to take the bull by the horns and conduct the interview on your terms.

You see where I'm going with this, don't you? That's good—because, in the final analysis, only practice and perfected pitching techniques can help you interview to win. But you can and will, even if you hate interviewing, because pitching is an integrated process, one that carries through your entire job-hunting process. (And then, of course, into your ongoing efforts to pitch yourself as a star after you have a job!) Once you get the hang of it—and, unless you emerge from the womb with the pitching prowess of our friend Hollie, which is rare—thinking on your feet during interviews will not only be painless, but fun. I, for instance, make a game out of trying to get jobs I have no desire to take, if only to keep my interviewing skills intact.

That said, neither I nor any other career counselor could ever prepare you for every possible question that might come your way during an interview. But that's fine, because as you've surely surmised, it's not the question itself, but the process of formulating an answer-as-pitch that's truly key. Once you've osmotically adapted this schema of thinking, you're home free.

Think of an interview as a performance. You can flub a few lines—nobody's perfect all the time—but if the overall feeling is there, you can still take home the award.

With that in mind, let's look at my Top Ten List of interview dos and don'ts.

1. Wear What You Look Best In

Happily, the days of Brooks-or-die outfitting are long gone. Even in investment banking firms, an Italian suit is acceptable— especially as upscale Americans are getting leaner all the time.

(Except in Congress, where baglike prep-suits are still the order of the day.) I'm not going to play Elsa Klensch and tell you what you should wear—quite frankly, I've rarely come across a candidate who didn't know how to dress in their field.

Of course, it goes without saying that you shouldn't get too wild, unless you're looking for something at a record company, hip magazine, or fashion manufacturer. Armani is fine; Gaultier is too outré for a Big Eight accounting firm. And yes, it's true that a prospective employer might not like what you're wearing (if you're in Armani and he bought his suit in Sears; or vice versa), but then you shouldn't be working there anyway.

Note to Gen Xers: Body piercings are cool, if slightly on their way out. But if you're looking to transcend the coffee house/video store/copy shop work syndrome, leave the nose ring at home. Okay?

2. Know Your Stuff

If you've read the company's annual report (where applicable) and know their products and services, you're two steps ahead of the game. With luck, you've also spotted articles on the organization in the business press and/or went to the library before the interview to locate same—now you're four giant steps ahead.

So relax—you're prepared. Some interviewees get manic, scrambling about for every arcane piece of information on the company they're interviewing for. Since you couldn't possibly be privy to inside information (unless you tried to seduce the president of the company or resort to similar subterfuge), you're not going to be given a pop quiz on this kind of minutiae. But don't come to the meeting in a daze, which many people do. At New Line, about 75 percent of candidates couldn't name a single film we'd distributed—and all they had to do was go to a video store, which is hardly international intrigue. Know the modicum about an organization, and you'll be fine.

3. Be on Time

Sound too stupid to say? Then consider this: In my experience, a good 25 percent of all applicants arrive late. In New York, the subway—which, admittedly, runs rather less frequently than when I was a lad—and in Los Angeles, the freeways are usually the scapegoats, but guess what: Neither excuse works. A job candidate who can't make the first meeting on time probably won't do so hot with the nine-to-five routine, methinks. Be there or be square!

4. Don't Interrupt

Of course you want to tell the world how fabulous you are; that's understandable. But in your zeal to pitch, don't appear overanxious; sit with a pleasant expression on your face, nodding occasionally (not like a bobbing clown on the dashboard of a low-rider's car), and speak only when your interviewer has made his or her point(s).

5. Be a Two-Minute Tootsie

It's easy to babble on incessantly, especially if the interviewer is ill prepared and lets the interview meander all over the place. And even if he or she is insightful and probing, short is always better. On the other hand, too short can also be a mistake (I myself tend to get terse and snittish when I feel the other party doesn't really care—kinda like being in a bar, no?) Two minutes is a good response time to most fairly involved questions, such as "Why don't you tell me about your responsibilities and accomplishments at your present job?" If you feel you really have more to say, end with, "And that, Bob, is my biggest accomplishment; I could tell you more if you had time." The ball is now in his court. If the interview is going well and Bob likes you, he'll probably ask you to tell him more; if not, he'll likely say, "Oh, no, that's all I need to know." After two minutes, always take your cue from the interviewer as to whether you should keep talking or make like the Sphinx.

6. Grab the Reins

In my experience, only about one out of four interviewers asks questions that are probing, intelligent, and on track. In this case, keep your wits about you and go with the flow. Quite frankly, well-planned interview sessions are so rare that I'm more than happy to let a smart questioner grill me to death. Superskilled interviews can be brainteasers of sorts, and I'm always up to the challenge. I have some clients who react negatively to high-pressure interviews, whereas I think they should feel happy to be weeded out, because if you can't stand the pressure during a thirty-minute interview, you'll certainly not be happy working for that firm.

In theory, the most dreaded question in interviewland is the banal and brainless "So . . . tell me about yourself." What it shows is an interviewer who: (a) hasn't spent two seconds looking at your résumé, a fact that is all too often representative of poor organizational skills—anathema to a hyper-anal-retentive freak like me; and/or (b) is too unimaginative to think of anything to say—another deal-killer for me, given that I require a modicum of conversational skills on the part of my boss (who, in many instances, you might actually have to sit on a plane with from time to time).

In fact, flippant guy that I am, when asked to "tell me about yourself," I can usually hardly resist a précis like: "In my spare time, I'm a male prostitute, drug dealer, and Nobel laureate in quantum physics" just to see if it gets a rise out of the dullard.

But hey—life is hard, and we all need to work. So when this question is posed to you (and it will be), take the bull by the horns and run with it. (But don't mix your metaphors like I have!) Instead, use this time to take an interviewer through your background with emphasis on the following:

- A *brief* nod to where you grew up (even if your childhood was ghastly, don't let on—unless you're interviewing to be on Sally Jessy or Geraldo). I myself paint a pastel picture of mint juleps on the shores of the Chesapeake, more than a slight exaggeration of the truth.

- Your education, with special focus on professional majors, internships, etc.

- Each job, citing responsibilities and achievements— always with a focus on your long-term directions (i.e., why you're facing the interviewer today).

- Any special skills that relate to the job at hand.

7. Be Enthusiastic!

Does this sound too trite for words? Maybe so, but it bears saying, because many job applicants whom I've interviewed acted like they'd rather be the subject of an *auto-da-fé* than sitting across from me. I'm not saying to act as fawning as the Nervous Nellie at the clothing company in the example above, but acting like the interview is less than total torture is a very good idea. Look bright-eyed, bushy-tailed, alert, and sit erect. Play the conversation like a hot tennis game: volley back and forth. Try to engage your listener, even if he or she hasn't immediately engaged you; even if your first blush isn't brilliant, you *can* turn an interview around. (Sometimes it's hitting on an area of mutual interest well outside the realm of work that can achieve this goal; if you discover a mutual adoration of Gregorian chant or wild boar hunting, milk it for all it's worth!)

8. Ask Good Questions

Again, these don't have to be superprobing because you can't possibly come armed with an inside knowledge of the company's most intimate operations or strategic plans. (You also don't want to show your interviewer up!) Instead, keep your line of questions at the medium-probe level, and try to steer this into a conversation of its own. As far as I'm concerned, it's easier to talk about whatever subject of mutual interest (personal or professional) you might happen to segue into rather than continue the barrage of questions you really don't want to ask and your interviewer would really rather not answer.

Note: The exception to this rule is when this is a second or third interview, a job for which you have an inside track (through a colleague or your own position within an organization), or have been given a synopsis of by a headhunter. In these instances, you may have relevant and intelligent questions that you may not only know to ask, but might actually need/want to have answered by the honcho in charge.

Lacking this inside info, the following general questions are always apropos:

(a) "As you can imagine, I'm rather familiar with the functions of this job, having held a similar post (or having done my research, etc.). But how, specifically, does this differ from other jobs in this field; what makes it unique?"

(b) "I'm most impressed by Company X's success to this point. What can you tell me about its future strategic plans, at least the ones you might disclose at this time?"

(c) "What kind of person works here? Can you narrow their foremost qualities down to two or three traits?"

(d) "What, if anything, in my background would give you cause for concern? Please let me know, because I'd like to reverse your attitude on these points, and show you why I'm just the right person for this job."

9. Ask for the Job

No, I don't mean on your hands and knees, but do remember to close the deal by letting your interviewer know how interested you are. As in: "Bob, I was very interested in joining Company X before we met today, and after our meeting I'm even more so. I feel that my unique blend of skills and achievements would allow me to do not just a good job here, but a great one.

I'm certainly very interested indeed, and hope we get the chance to continue our discussions about this job."

10. Follow Up

Refer to the sections on follow-up pitches on pages 113–118 to take your interest to the nth degree and remind prospective employers just how great you really are.

18
· · ·

The Perfect Freelance/ Consulting Pitch or Downsized but Not Out!

Whether you're a reluctant freelancer (by dint of the ever-growing trend of "work-for-hire" author Meyer describes) or the daredevil high-risk type who thrives on working project by project, the chances are you're getting your work by the seat of your pants.

I'd say that as much as 90 percent of freelance workers operate without anything resembling an organized, strategic business plan. This is because:

1. In fatter times (remember the eighties?), many "free-lancers"—and by that I mean small business owners, professionals in specialized fields, and individual workers alike—didn't have to ferret out work endlessly; it came right to them. In the late nineties, with smaller corporate budgets, scads of downsized employees, and an

overall "lean and mean" mentality in corporate America, this is no longer the case.

2. Many people in fields where searching for work is an ongoing process tend to adopt a passive, come-what-may attitude that, if left unchecked, can ultimately result in their financial and professional demise. This is, I believe, a natural extension of the deus ex machina syndrome I noted in the early chapter on organizing your personal pitch. If I had a dollar for every time I heard lines like "Things will work themselves out" and "The universe is a friendly place," I'd be a rich bloke indeed. Certainly, it's a lovely thought, and many self-help authors have made millions espousing such views. Unfortunately, such passive (if positive) thinking doesn't do much when the bill man is on your case.

3. It's just too much work.

In the latter camp, I offer two cases in point. The first is my dearest, oldest friend who is brilliant, beautiful, and a supertalented writer to boot. She currently writes two high-profile newspaper fashion columns for which she works her butt off and takes home less pay than the average secretary in Manhattan. She needs to do two things, and to do them fast:

(a) *Pitch like the devil.* To make more money, you need more jobs, whatever your area of expertise may be. Take stock of how much time you're spending on projects, what the financial rewards are, and where you should be concentrating your time. But the bottom line is this:

If you're not making enough money, you need to spend more time pitching new business.

(Does this sound simplistic? Then consider this: of clients I counsel, only about one in ten does what I consider to be a decent job of sourcing and pitching new clients on an ongoing, long-term basis.)

(b) *Make your name known.* Remember the section on promoting yourself in the corporate world in Chapter 12? Take that advice and double it, and you'll have an idea of how important this is for individuals working on their own. (Specific pitches to the press are provided later in this chapter.)

In my friend's case, she should be garnering publicity by promoting herself as an authority on beauty and fashion for the zillions of talk and local news shows in New York and beyond. All this would take is a simple press release to the producers in charge. (How do you think those other people—experts in scores of fields—get on those shows? True, some of them have publicists, but most of them can't afford professional media placement, and do the work themselves.) But she hasn't done this, and daily sees lesser writers' mugs on camera.

Here's the other example I wanted to share. I'm presently counseling a medium-sized design and advertising agency whose billings have been slipping downward from the previous years. The first apparent attitude is a variation on the theme of sour grapes: "How does such-and-such agency get so much work? We have much better designs than they do."

Truer words may never have been spoken, but just like in full-time job search, it's not just what you know and what you can do, but how many doors you knock on and how you position your skills. So, of course, the first question I asked this client is the old classic: "What are you doing to get new business?"

His response—almost unbelievably, the one I usually hear: "Nothing."

There you have it folks, amazing but true: *Most people don't get enough freelance work because they just don't look hard enough.*

You'd think the opposite, wouldn't you? That, despite their best efforts and sublime pitching campaigns, the reason people are underemployed is that there just isn't enough work to go around. Well, I'm here to tell you that in most fields in most places in this country, that just ain't true.

There are some exceptions, of course. Architects and academics in many specialties could pitch from now until doomsday, but there just aren't enough jobs to go around. But those fields are the exception rather than the rule, so I'll say again: There's work to be had if you're willing to exert enough effort to find it.

So what about the ad agency I mentioned above?

"People know us as an entertainment agency. I don't think anybody would use us in other industries," the CEO said.

"Why not?" I asked.

"Oh, you know, people just get ideas in their heads about what you can do."

"I see, and these ideas are immutable concepts, impossible to change?"

"Well, no, not necessarily. But it's just easier to stay in your field."

"Granted, it's easier. But your bills are piled up, and you need to generate work. From what you've said, you've already had your account people scour the entertainment industry, and you're not getting the work you need. So isn't it time to cast your eye on other areas?"

"I guess. But you know, L.A. is a one-industry town."

"That's a cliché that's no longer true. Though I'll give you this: It's the favorite drug for clients of mine who are looking for full-time work and don't want to expend the energy to look outside that field."

"So you're saying I'm lazy?"

"Nope, you said it. But I agree. By the way, you'd be a lot less sluggish without the three glasses of wine at lunch."

"Yeah, well, it takes my mind off things."

"I can well imagine. But right now, my friend, your mind needs to be *on* things—especially on building your business."

"So what can I do?"

"*First, define your targets.*" (Yes, reader, as with your personal plan for an on-staff job, delineating your goals is key for freelance and consulting work.) "Now, my first thought is this: You referred to a one-industry town. But of all the cities in the U.S., Los Angeles is the most spread-out megalopolis, so you should set your sights wide. After all, what is L.A. County but an amalgam of townships and virtual city-states: Santa Monica, West Hollywood, Beverly Hills, Glendale, Burbank, Culver City, etc. And what about the Valley, the South Bay, the Inland Empire? There are tons of companies throughout southern California, and you've barely scratched the surface."

(Note: although L.A. is probably the best example of how far you can spread your sights, no city anywhere is immune to such a view. Consider expanding your horizons to neighboring counties, the next biggest city, or entire regions, say the Midwest as a whole. Only the limits of your industry and logistical realities should limit your scope. *In all cases, follow the same format I discuss for full-time job seekers in Chapter 6 to define the scope of your freelance search.*)

"Second, define your goals. What kind of work are you looking for?" (This, of course, should be based on a careful examination of your own strengths, as well as current needs in a variety of industries, the result of ongoing, never-ending research.) "Do your target companies only need ads? What about logo design? Merchandise displays? The more specific and targeted your pitch, the greater your chance of success in landing an assignment.

"Third, conjure up the best possible plan of attack. How do you plan to garner new clients: By direct mail? Attending trade shows? Referrals? Placing an ad? Cold calling?"

Here, my client interrupted me: "Well, we can't afford advertising the agency; it's too expensive."

"That well may be. But you've done none of the other prospecting I just mentioned, either. In effect, you've closed the door on new business without giving much thought as to how you could procure it."

"Yeah, that's true. It just all seems like so much work."

"Of course it's work. That's part and parcel of having your own business. In the corporate world, it's much easier to veg out and do the modicum, even in these downsized times. When you work for yourself, you have to hustle every second of the day—and that I can tell you firsthand."

"Okay, so I guess I have to be a little more productive, but I'm not happy about it. When I started this company, I had people coming to me."

"And so do many other freelancers and consultants—at least at first. But anyone who thinks this kind of job is a carefree bed of roses has got it all wrong. Yes, you may leave a corporate job with a bevy of clients, but two things are true: You'll always come away with less than you thought you'd have—promises, promises, right? And then, regardless of your initial client base, it's a well that requires constant replenishment; so if you're not willing to find the continuing source, you'd better give up illusions of the freelance life posthaste."

"All right, I get it. But can we start tomorrow?"

"I think that's a good idea, because I can see that the wine is putting you to sleep. But remember this: The longer you procrastinate, the better the chance that someone else is getting your work. In any case, I'm not going to force this down your throat. If you really want to start tomorrow, leave a message on my machine by the end of the day. I'd love to help you, but you have to take the first step. In the meantime, I've done my prospecting, so I have plenty to work on if you'd rather wait."

"Very funny. Despite the wine, I catch the sarcasm."

"Good. It was about as subtle as a ton of bricks. See you tomorrow . . . I hope."

I'll be honest: Because I have an almost puritanical work ethic, procrastination and laziness drive me up the wall. I can understand not getting new business because there's too much competition, because a business is badly conceived, or because corporate funds are sere. But I can't for the life of me understand how people can just not get work because they're not willing to put out the work required. Times are tough, to be sure; but getting work, whether full time or freelance, is possible if you just put out the effort required and focus your attention in the right direction!

• • •

Happily, my agency friend called me before the end of the afternoon to confirm our appointment for the following day.

The next morning, we met in his office over French roast. (Downsizing may be the office scourge of the nineties, but the general improvement in office coffee is, conversely, a most welcome trend!)

"I'm psyched," he told me. "Let's give this new business thing one last try!"

"Whoa, kiddo. I'm pleased to proceed, but before I do so, I have something important to say. This isn't 'your last try' for two reasons: first, because you've never actually conducted a concerted campaign before. Second, and most important, even if you should secure scores of new clients, this will in no shape or form be your last new client pitch. No matter how many new customers you get and how much publicity you should receive, pitching is an ongoing project for every freelancer, consultant, and owner of business large and small."

"Whew. You're a slave driver! Well, let's just take one step at a time."

"Fine. Let's begin with the beginning. Who are your targets, and where are they?"

Note: It doesn't really matter whether you start with this question or the second point above, that is, how you're positioning yourself as a freelancer/consultant. In fact, often, the two questions are inextricably part of the same equation, so don't fret about the order; that you address and answer both issues is of prime importance here.

"Well, that's what I need help with. I just keep thinking that other industries wouldn't give us the time of day because we've done so much entertainment work."

"I take exception to that on two counts. First, because I don't accept that fatalistic, 'no-can-do' attitude from anyone. Second, and much more important, is this: Isn't all advertising supposed to be entertaining—or, at the very least, disruptive and diverting?"

"Well, of course! That's what they teach you in design school." Trevor laughed.

"Precisely. And you've done award-winning design ads for movie studios and record companies—the kind of high-profile stuff a company in any field would find sexy."

"Yes, but maybe they wouldn't get it."

"So guess what, big guy—you have to tell them. *Making them 'get it' is what pitching is all about!*"

(Remember the story of Jodie, who had all the skills necessary for a career change but didn't know how to sell herself? The same situation is repeating itself in this tale.)

"After all," I continued, "for an ad agency, the client's field is less important than understanding what the company does and how to design ads and supporting materials that sell the product or service."

"Right . . . but how do we let prospective clients know that?"

"Do you have a brochure or 'leave-behind' of any kind?"

"Well, no; we've never needed one."

"That's ironic, since you're in the communication field. Guess what? You're going to need one, along with a pitch letter to sell your firm. But we'll get to that later. For now, we have to think about whom you're going to target."

"That's the thing, Dave. [My clients always call me Dave, even though my friends never do. I've been looking for a fifties bowling shirt with *Dave* emblazoned on it for about ten years, to no avail.] I don't know how to find clients in other fields."

"That, my friend, is called research. And it's something you're going to have to learn to do."

"Oh, God, I always hated to do research in school. Can't I pay you to do it for me?"

"Of course you can, but it would cost you a bundle . . . and besides, it would only accentuate your basically lazy nature. It's a project you might give to your account execs; though, honestly, if I were you, I'd do it myself."

"So where do I go for this information?"

(At this juncture, readers, you should refer back to "Developing Your Personal Perfect Pitch" in Chapter 6 to determine how to research and amass a key target list. Freelancers and business owners might also want to consider buying company lists from direct mail brokers, though these can range from decent to dismal, depending. Compiling target lists on your own is always your best bet.)

"Now, let's fast-forward a bit. You've put together a dynamite target list; but what's your best plan of attack?"

"Mailing them a brochure, I guess. Isn't that what you were talking about?"

"Yes and no. Direct mail is, in most cases, a keystone of wide-target attacks, but it's hardly the only way to reach prospective clients."

"I know—but remember, I can't afford to place ads."

"That's what many people say, and certainly advertising for clients should never be your only mode of attack. So let's sidestep this issue right now, but let me just say this: When we talk about advertising, we're not talking about the *L.A. Times.* Placing small display ads in trade magazines can be cheaper than you think."

"All right, well, let's come back to that."

"Sure. Now one of our target industries is the interactive/high-tech area, which abounds in the state of California. Is there any forum at which these companies might gather, so that they in effect come to us in one place, rather than our ferreting them out one by one?"

"Um, let's see . . . well, I know of at least one big trade show, called E-3, that takes place once a year right here in L.A."

"That's a great start . . . but let's not leave a single stone unturned. You may not have the answer now, but make a note—no, not a mental note, get out your pen and write this down!—to find out where the other regional trade shows take place, and when."

"Okay, so we go to the trade show. What then?"

"You have any number of choices. You or your account reps can 'do' the show, and chat up company members who are in the booth. Even if they don't have time to talk then and there, you can at least find out who the key people are, and follow up by calling or writing, saying 'Meeting you at the E-3 Show was a great pleasure indeed, et cetera, et cetera.' You may not have to spend much time talking to them, but at least you've got a slight 'in' there."

Note: I'd be less than honest if I told you that, when cruising trade shows, it's not a tremendous help to be good-looking and gregarious. Looks sell, and that's a fact. If you're not a "people person," that's okay—you don't have to talk to someone at every booth, only to those who seem immediately unharried and receptive. And, at the very least, you can always pick up the show's membership directory, a fabulous compendium of who's who in that industry.

Even if you don't talk to tons of people at trade shows, this is a great opportunity to pick up promotional literature on the various attendees, which will allow you to make specialized pitches like this:

Mr. Lucas Lyons
TechStyles Inc.
111 El Nerdo Way
Sunnyvale, CA 99999

Dear Mr. Lyons:

Great to meet you—albeit briefly!—at the E-3 Show in Los Angeles last week. I was thrilled to see the packaging for the new Soldier Stan CD-ROMs; from every angle, it looks to be one of the big introductions for Christmas '98.

And I can make it an even bigger one!

As a promotional consultant in the interactive game field, I have created and implemented store promos for some of the biggest launches ever, including the Toys 'R' Us introduction of Wired for Sound that resulted in a 43 percent increase in store traffic! (I've also worked for TechnoToys, Z-12 Plus, and other top industry names.)

A brief work history is enclosed for your review, but that's just the tip of my creative iceberg. I'll call to see if I can't tell you more soon.

Best regards,

Seth O'Malley

Or, in the case of my advertising client:

Dear Mr. Lyons:

I was delighted to see your plans for the Soldier Stan intro coming up this year. When it comes to new product innovations, your company truly leads the way!

Of course, that's how we at JBC Advertising feel, too. Whether we're designing a poster for a major movie studio or packaging for one of our interactive clients, our credo is always the same: that nothing less than an award-winning, eye-catching design will do.

The enclosed brochure and design samples tell you more. May we meet so I can tell you the whole story soon?

I'll call to set up a time that's good for you. Till then, thank you for thinking of JBC.

Best and thanks,

Trevor Goodwin
President

You've seen then, how freelancers can target and pitch prospective clients in very much the same way as do people looking for full-time jobs. With one very big difference: Unlike on-staff job hunters, whose efforts have a finite focus, pitching is, for freelancers and consultants, an ongoing part of their jobs. Many folks retreat to the corporate world as soon as it's possible, and who can blame them? The freelancer's universe can be a very shaky place. But for those of us who thrive on taking risks, are supersure of our abilities, and love the thrill of a brand-new (unexplored!) day, the rewards can be rich indeed—*if* you remember that pitching is a continual and integral, never merely auxiliary, part of each day's work.

The Personal Perfect Pitch for Freelancers/Consultants

You've seen in Chapter 7 how on-staff workers can become stars by promoting themselves using in-house newsletters, status reports, and trade magazines. Now, let's look at how you can pitch to win exposure for your own freelance and small business expertise.

Pitch Trade Magazines

As with full-time employees, garnering mentions in the trade press is much easier that you'd think. Why? Because unlike consumer magazines, whose editors are constantly beleaguered by publicists trying to get their clients, products, and services in the pages of, say, *People, Vogue,* or *Rolling Stone,* the much less sexy trade periodicals are mere repositories for any and all information on the industries they represent. While they certainly favor advertisers and big companies in the field, being mentioned—or even receiving "top billing" as the focus of a whole article—is no Herculean task. This is true because trade publication editors are, quite frankly, hungry for information and suggestions for story ideas. So if you have something novel to say or can suggest a new slant for a story, coverage of you (and your business or service) is virtually guaranteed.

Here's a step-by-step guide on what to do:

(a) Amass a list of trade publications in your field.

(b) Call and find out the name of the editor-in-chief.

(c) Thoroughly peruse each publication (in most industries, there are no more than two or three, so this isn't quite the undertaking it would seem) and analyze what kind of stories they run, what their regular columns are, and what their special features are about. Consider the issues that are most topical to your industry or field in today's market. Then, position yourself in such a way that makes sense to the publication.

Some examples to consider:

• An accountant proposed a story in which he rated the efficacy of a range of mass-market computer accounting programs for use by professionals and amateurs alike.

• A boutique owner suggested a short roundup of the newest fabrics for a textile magazine, featuring exact quotes from her customers as to their likes and dislikes—plus retail sales of each fabric type.

• A sales rep with a major packaged goods company wrote a feature on new merchandising techniques and consumer sales programs for the leading grocery chain magazine.

Is this stuff as sexy as a Sharon Stone pictorial in *Harper's Bazaar*? Hell, no! Does it get you noticed by the major players in your field? You better believe the answer is yes! Does it require slightly more effort than maintaining the internal force of the status quo? Again, I tell you yes. But whether you choose to be a de facto authority in your field or a shy lily of the valley is also entirely up to you.

How to approach the editor of a trade newsletter or magazine? You don't have to be Willie Shakespeare; a letter that's short, simple, and specific will do just fine. Like this one:

Ms. Paige Planner
Editor-in-Chief
GROCERY NEWS
333 Bagboy Way
Decatur, GA 33333

Dear Ms. Planner:

You and I both know contests and promotions are seen every day in grocery and drug chains across the land.

But do they really work?

As regional sales representative for Major Food Groups, Inc., I vote an unequivocal yes. And here's why: I've been implementing successful in-store merchandising campaigns for over four years. But to achieve a sales-busting program, you have to know what works, and what promotions sit in stores like a ton of lead.

I propose a one-page feature story on my tips of the trade for *Grocery News.* In this article, I will delineate the key aspects of a successful store promotion, as well as the pitfalls and missteps that can lead a promotion to the road to ruin.

I'll call soon to discuss this and other ideas with you. Till then, my thanks.

Cordially,

Leonard Lunch

P.S. As an expert in the field, I'd be happy to provide quotes for future stories on the grocery business. To that end, I'm enclosing my business card; won't you please keep me in mind? Thanks.

You'll note, of course, that Leonard has not only sealed the deal of the pitch by promising to follow up, but he has actually sweetened the deal by offering himself as an authority in the field. As with all pitches, "If at first you don't succeed . . . " is the operative motto; even if his first story pitch doesn't work, he should try again, and reoffer his services as an authority in the field for stories that other people write. Don't be afraid to come back swingin': Unlike consumer magazines, where getting a story placed or obtaining a publicity mention can be a bear-and-a-half, trade publication editors will usually bend over backwards to be nice to people working in the field. (After all, who knows when you'll be in position to place an ad, or will be a major player whom they'll be begging for a quote?)

The bottom line: If a trade editor senses you're serious and sincere, he or she will be more than willing to be of help. But do take note: As long as you can string grammatical sentences together over the course of two pages, anything you write will be fine. If, however, you know that English syntax and grammar are not your strength, ask a friend or colleague to give what you've written a glance. As I said before, your piece doesn't have to be Pulitzer quality, but it should be cogent, proofread, and neat to the eye.

"But David," I hear you ask, "why should I bother when

everyone else reading this book will be doing exactly the same thing?" The answer is easy: Because, my friends, not everyone else *will* bother. Even among my clients, everyone nods their head eagerly, but most people quickly drop the ball. Remember what I said earlier? When it comes to pitching, it's not always the textbook brightest who succeed beyond their wildest dreams, but those who are bright and brilliant like stars. Woody Allen once said (one of my favorite quotes ever!), "Eighty percent of success is just showing up." So you don't have to be a world-class writer or thinker to get publicity for yourself; to quote the Nike slogan, "Just do it," and you'll succeed.

Pitch the Consumer Press

This is, in all candor, legions more difficult than working your name into trade publications, but for seasoned pitchers it's all part of the game. Now, let's be honest: If you're a sales rep for a food company, neither *People* nor *Playboy* will be interested in you, and MTV will not be beating a path to your door.

There are, however, two media outlets that may well be interested in what you have to say. These are the business and/or lifestyle section of your major metropolitan newspaper, and consumer business magazines like *Business Week, Inc.,* the *Wall Street Journal, Black Enterprise,* etc. If you're not familiar with those publications most apropos to you and your career, you should be; waltz over to a newsstand or bookstore immediately and buy those that look most germane to what you do. Peruse them as you did the trade publications and decide how you might fit in.

Specifically: What do you do better than anyone else? What unique service do you provide? What new trend is happening in your field? If you can't answer these questions, you shouldn't bother to write; but if you come up with novel attitudes, techniques, or slants, then fire away!

As with the trade magazines, write directly to the editor-in-chief. For the smaller publications, your letter may strike an immediate chord; otherwise, he or she will pass it on to the appropriate editor in whose jurisdiction your specialty or idea falls. Once you become a real pro at this, you can expand your horizons to (as in the letter below) business editors for non-business magazines.

Here's an example from my personal files:

Mr. Greg Ptacek
Business Editor
Men's Fitness
333 Sepulveda Street
Los Angeles, CA 99999

Dear Mr. Ptacek:

In these downsized times, it seems that many people are running for their professional lives.

When it rains, it pours; what a great time it is to be a career counselor! And as one of the best—and the author of the soon-to-be-published Warner Book, *THE PERFECT PITCH: How to Sell Yourself for Today's Job Market*—I can offer insights of definite interest to readers of your magazine.

Should you elect to interview me for your column, I could talk about such topics as:

(a) Where downsizing is most likely to continue to occur—and who will be spared.

(b) The first three things to do when you've lost your job.

(c) How my techniques of the "perfect pitch" can make the difference between finding a job fast and languishing in the unemployment line.

A sample chapter from my book and past press on me are enclosed for your review. I'll call soon to see what you think.

Best and thanks,

David Andrusia
Author, *THE PERFECT PITCH*
(Warner Books, 1997)

P.S. My business card is enclosed. Won't you keep me on file as an eminent authority in the career counseling field? Kind thanks.

As my letter illustrates, it's not enough to merely say "Here I am!"; you must be very specific as to what you can bring to the party—the unique and topical viewpoint you'll share with readers of the newspaper or magazine. Moreover, always remember to seal the deal by calling the editor back, a tactic every ace publicist would endorse. Be prepared to return the call several times if you get voice mail; editors are besieged by publicists all day, every day. If, after several attempts, you don't get a call back, put this on the back burner, but never fail to recontact that editor with a story idea later on.

On the other hand, if you're lucky (and persistent!) enough to speak to that editor, you may find out that he or she isn't interested in exactly the slant you suggest, but may well use you (now or later) for another story. Seeking out and fostering relationships with editors is key to consultants and freelancers who truly know their Perfect Pitch.

19
· · ·

Persistence:
The Truly Perfect Pitch

As I write these closing pages, the Summer Olympics are coming to a close. Like everyone else in the world, I've been glued to the set for two solid weeks (using archery—snore!—as my preferred bathroom break).

It's fitting, then, that I should be touched by a theme running through so many athletes' lives: that of persistence, of never giving up. Oh sure, the media milk that "triumph over tragedy" stuff to an almost nauseating degree—"That's it, Bob! Walter Winsome has won the gold medal in discus despite suffering from the heartbreak of halitosis for twenty-five years!" Almost, but not totally, because the ability to "keep on keepin' on" is the common thread all athletes share—and is an inspirational motto we all should share.

Pitching may not be an Olympic sport—at least not yet!—but the ways and means are the same. I've tried my damnedest (and, hopefully, triumphed over adversity—I wrote this book with a hangnail!) to drive home one superimportant point: that perfection in pitching doesn't just happen once; it's an ongoing

process, a lifetime thing. That's the secret the world's most successful people share, and it's the one you'll come to cherish as
you pitch to win—now, and in the years to come!

Upward and onward!

My very best,

David Anderson

Appendix

Employment Reference Sources

A first-rate target list is a crucial component of your pitch; make yours perfect by identifying every possible employer in your field. Developing an A-list is fine, but unless your target roster is as close to all-encompassing as possible, you're missing key people and places who might just be your next boss and employer. At the risk of overkill, let me tell you again how many of my clients miss the boat—and, just maybe, the job of their dreams—by compiling target lists that are anything less than 100 percent complete. (Or, even worse, who amass great target lists, then don't pitch.) When it comes to looking for work, be it freelance or on staff, "good enough" never is!

The following is a compendium of references in major industries and fields. It is an excellent starting point for amassing a target list, but don't let it be your final destination. As I've said repeatedly in this book, becoming intimately acquainted with your industry's trade associations and publications is a vital part of your lifetime Perfect Pitch. Always remember to call your field's trade publications (the advertising department is usually best; if not, contact the editorial staff) to ask where you can find a directory of companies or organizations in your field before giving the stamp of approval to your target list.

Finally, remember that these directories tend to be expensive (as well they should be—their compilation is a Herculean task). Unless you've got Trump-sized assets, call several libraries in your area to find out if they have the guide(s) you need. If you must buy one or more of these directories, call and ask for a brochure or sales sheet on each in order to ascertain they have the exact kind(s) of information you need. Most important of all: Be sure the guide you're using is the very latest, and always call to confirm titles and positions for organizations on your top target list.

General Business

Dun's Career Guide
Dun's Marketing Services
3 Sylvan Way
Parsippany, NJ 07054

Hoover's Handbook of American Business
The Reference Press
6448 Highway 290 East
Suite E-104
Austin, TX 78723
800/486-8666

Hoover's Handbook of Emerging Companies
The Reference Press
6448 Highway 290 East
Suite E-104
Austin, TX 78723
800/486-8666

Macmillan Directory of Leading Private Companies
Reed Reference Publishing
121 Chanlon Road
New Providence, NJ 07974
800/521-8110

Peterson's Job Opportunities for
Liberal Arts Graduates
Peterson's Guides, Inc.
P.O. Box 2123
Princeton, NJ 08543
609/243-9111

Standard Directory of Advertisers
National Register
Publishing Co., Inc.
3004 Glenview Road
Wilmette, IL 60091
800/323-6727
708/441-2210 (in Illinois)

Accounting

Accountants Directory
American Business
Directories, Inc.
5711 S. 86th Circle
P.O. Box 27347
Omaha, NE 68127
402/593-4600

American Institute of Certified
Public Accountants
Firm on Firm Directory
Harborside Financial Center
201 Plaza 3
Jersey City, NJ 07311
201/938-3000

National Directory of Accounting
Firms and Accountants
Gale Research, Inc.
835 Penobscot Building
Detroit, MI 48226
800/877-GALE

Advertising

AAAA Roster
American Association of
Advertising Agencies
666 Third Avenue
New York, NY 10017
212/682-2500

Macmillan Directory of
International Advertisers
and Agencies
Reed Reference Publishing
121 Chanlon Road
New Providence, NJ 07974
800/521-8110

Standard Directory of
Advertising Agencies
Reed Reference Publishing
121 Chanlon Road
New Providence, NJ 07974
800/521-8110

Aerospace

Aerospace Facts and Figures
Aerospace Industries Association
1250 I St., NW
Washington, D.C. 20005
202/371-8500

World Aviation Directory
Aviation Week Group
McGraw-Hill, Inc.
1200 G St., NW
Washington, D.C. 20005
202/383-3700

Apparel

American Apparel
Manufacturers Association
2500 Wilson Boulevard
Arlington, VA 22201
703/524-1864

Clothing Manufacturers
Association of the USA
1290 Avenue of the Americas
New York, NY 10104
212/757-6664

Davison's Textile Blue Book
Davison Publishing Co.
P.O. Box 477
Ridgewood, NJ 07451
201/445-3135

International Association of
Clothing Designers
475 Park Avenue South
New York, NY 10016
212/685-6602

Artists, Illustrators, Designers

American Art Directory
Reed Reference Publishing
121 Chanlon Road
New Providence, NJ 07074
800/521-8110

Artist's Market
Writer's Digest Books
1507 Dana Avenue
Cincinnati, OH 45207
513/531-2222

Creative Black Book
Macmillan Creative
Services Group
115 Fifth Avenue
New York, NY 10003
212/254-1330

Design Firm Directory
Wefler & Associates
P.O. Box 1167
Evanston, IL 60204
708/475-1866

Graphic Arts Blue Book
A. F. Lewis and Co., Inc.
79 Madison Avenue
New York, NY 10016
212/679-0770

Automotive

The Market Data Book
Crain Communications
1400 Woodbridge Avenue
Detroit, MI 48207
313/446-6000

Ward's Automotive Yearbook
Ward's Communications, Inc.
28 W. Adams Street
Detroit, MI 48226
313/962-4433

Aviation

Official Airline Guide
2000 Clearwater Drive
Oak Brook, IL 60521
800/323-3537

World Aviation Directory
McGraw-Hill, Inc.
1200 G. St., NW
Washington, D.C. 20005
202/383-3700

Banking

American Bank Directory
McFadden Business Publications
6195 Crooked Creek Road
Norcross, GA 30092
404/448-1011

American Banker Yearbook
American Banker, Inc.
1 State Street Plaza
New York, NY 10003
212/803-6700

*Moody's Bank and
Financial Manual*
99 Church Street
New York, NY 10007
212/553-0300

Polk's Bank Directory
R. L. Polk & Co.
P.O. Box 3051000
Nashville, TN 37230
800/827-2265

Broadcasting

Broadcasting & Cable Marketplace
P.O. Box 31
New Providence, NJ 07974
800/323-4345

Broadcasting Yearbook
Broadcasting
Publications, Inc.
1705 DeSales St., NW
Washington, D.C. 20036
202/659-2340

World Radio TV
Handbook
Billboard Publications
1515 Broadway
New York, NY 10036
212/764-7300

Chemicals

Chemicals Directory
275 Washington St.
Newton, MA 02158
617/964-3030

Directory of Chemical
Producers
Stanford Research Institute
333 Ravenswood Avenue
Menlo Park, CA 94025
415/859-3627

Computers

Directory of Top
Computer Executives
Applied Computer Research
P.O. Box 82266
Phoenix, AZ 85071
602/995-5929

Information Industry
Directory
Gale Research, Inc.
835 Penobscot Building
Detroit, MI 48226
800/877-GALE

Consumer Goods

Electronic Market
Data Book
2001 Pennsylvania Ave., NW
Washington, D.C. 20006
202/457-4900

Household and
Personal Products Industry
Buyers Guide
Rodman Publishing
17 S. Frankling Turnpike
Ramsey, NJ 07446
201/825-2552

Engineering

Directory of Engineers in
Private Practice
National Society of
Professional Engineers
1420 King Street
Alexandria, VA 22314
703/684-2800

Peterson's Job Opportunities
for Engineering, Science, and
Computer Graduates
Peterson's Guides, Inc.
P.O. Box 2123
Princeton, NJ 08543
609/243-9111

Entertainment

Hollywood Reporter
Blu-Book
5055 Wilshire Boulevard #600
Los Angeles, CA 90036
213/525-2000

Who's Who in the Motion
Picture Industry
Packard Publishing
P.O. Box 2187
Beverly Hills, CA 90213
213/854-0276

Financial

Corporate Finance Sourcebook
Reed Reference Publishing
121 Chanlon Road
New Providence, NJ 07974
800/323-6772

Moody's Bank & Finance Manual
Moody's Investor Service
99 Church Street
New York, NY 10007
212/553-0300

Securities Industry Yearbook
120 Broadway
New York, NY 10271
212/608-1500

Food and Beverage

American Frozen Food
Industry Directory
1746 Old Meadow Lane
McLean, VA 22102
703/821-0770

Hereld's 5000: The Directory of
Leading U.S. Food, Confectionery,
Beverage, and Pet Food
Manufacturers
200 Leeder Hill Drive
Hamden, CT 06517
203/281-6766

Jobson's Handbook
100 Avenue of the Americas
New York, NY 10013
212/274-7000

Health Care and Services

AHA Guide to the
Health Care Field
American Hospital Association
1840 N. Lake Shore Drive
Chicago, IL 60611
800/621-6902

Billians Hospital Blue Book
2100 Powers Ferry Road
Atlanta, GA 30339
404/955-5656

Dun's Guide to Health Care
Companies
Dun's Marketing Services
3 Sylvan Way
Parsippany, NJ 07054
201/605-6000

Hospital Phone Book
Reed Reference Publishing
121 Chanlon Road
New Providence, NJ 07974
800/521-8110

Nursing Career Directory
Springhouse Corp.
1111 Bethlehem Pike
Springhouse, PA 19477
215/646-8700

U.S. Medical Directory
Reed Reference Publishing
121 Chanlon Road
New Providence, NJ 07974
800/521-8110

Hospitality

Chain Restaurant Operators
Lebhar-Friedman, Inc.
425 Park Avenue
New York, NY 10022
212/756-5000

Dun's Guide to
Healthcare Companies
Dun's Marketing Services
3 Sylvan Way
Parsippany, NJ 07054
800/526-0651
201/605-6000 in NJ

Food Service
Industry Directory
National Restaurant Association
1200 17th Street, NW
Washington, D.C. 20036
202/331-5900

Hotel and Motel Red Book
American Hotel Association
Directory Corp.
1201 New York Avenue, NW
Washington, D.C. 20005
202/289-3162

Insurance

Insurance Almanac
Underwriting Printing &
Publishing Co.
50 E. Palisades Avenue
Englewood, NJ 07631

Insurance Phone
Book and Directory
Reed Reference Publishing
121 Chanlon Road
New Providence, NJ 07974
800/323-6772

Law

Law Firm Yellow Pages
Monitor Publishing Co.
104 Fifth Avenue
New York, NY 10011
212/627-4140

Martindale-Hubbell Law Directory
Martindale-Hubbell, Inc.
P.O. Box 1001
Summit, NJ 07902
800/526-4902
201/464-6800 (in NJ)

Manufacturing

American Manufacturers Directory
American Business Directories
5711 S. 86th Circle
Omaha, NE 68127
402/593-4600

Moody's Industrial Manual
99 Church Street
New York, NY 10007
212/553-0300

Thomas Register of American
Manufacturers
Thomas Publishing Company
1 Penn Plaza
New York, NY 10119
212/290-7200

Metals

Directory of Iron
and Steel Plants
3 Gateway Center, Suite 2350
Pittsburgh, PA 15222
412/281-6323

Iron and Steel
Works Directory
American Iron and Steel
Institute
1101 17th St., NW
Washington, D.C. 20036
202/452-7100

Nonprofit Organizations

The Foundation Directory
The Foundation Center
79 Fifth Avenue
New York, NY 10003
212/620-4230

National Directory of
Nonprofit Organizations
The Taft Group
12300 Twinbrook Parkway
Rockville, MD 20852
301/816-0210

Oil

Oil & Gas Directory
P.O. Box 130508
Houston, TX 77219
713/529-8789

Paper/Forest Products

Directory of the Forest
Products Industry
Miller Freeman Publications
6600 Silacci Way
Gilroy, CA 95020
408/848-5296

International Pulp
and Paper Directory
Miller Freeman Publications
6600 Silacci Way
Gilroy, CA 95020
408/848-5296

Pharmaceuticals

Pharmaceutical Marketers
Directory
CPS Communications
7200 West Camino Real
Boca Raton, FL 33433
407/368-9301

Public Relations

O'Dwyer's Directory of
Corporate Communications
271 Madison Avenue
New York, NY 10016
212/679-2471

O'Dwyer's Directory of
Public Relations Firms
271 Madison Avenue
New York, NY 10016
212/679-2471

Public Relations
Consultants Directory
American Business Directories,
Inc.
5707 S. 86th Circle
Omaha, NE 68127
402/331-7169

Publishing

American Book Trade Directory
Reed Reference Publishing
121 Chanlon Road
New Providence, NJ 07974
800/521-8110

Bacon's Publicity Checker
Bacon's Publishing Co.
332 S. Michigan Avenue
Chicago, IL 60604

Editor & Publisher
International Yearbook
11 West 19th Street
New York, NY 10011
212/675-4380

Gale Directory of Publications
Gale Research, Inc.
835 Penobscot Building
Detroit, MI 48226
800/877-4253

Literary Marketplace
Directory of American
Book Publishing
Reed Reference Publishing
121 Chanlon Road
New Providence, NJ 07974
800/521-8110

Magazine Industry
Marketplace
Reed Reference Publishing
121 Chanlon Road
New Providence, NJ 07974
800/521-8110

National Directory of Magazines
Oxbridge Communications
150 Fifth Avenue
New York, NY 10011
212/741-0231

Publishers Directory
Gale Research, Inc.
835 Penobscot Building
Detroit, MI 48226
800/877-4253

Real Estate

Real Estate Sourcebook
Reed Reference Publishing
121 Chanlon Road
New Providence, NJ 07974
800/323-6772

Retailing

Directory of Department Stores
Chain Store Guide
Information Services
425 Park Avenue
New York, NY 10022
212/756-5252

*Directory of General
Merchandise/Specialty Stores*
Chain Store Guide
Information Services
425 Park Avenue
New York, NY 10022
212/756-5252

*Fairchild's Financial Manual
of Retail Stores*
Fairchild Publications
7 West 34th Street
New York, NY 10001
800/247-6622

Scientific Fields

*Peterson's Job Opportunities
for Engineering, Science, and
Computer Graduates*
Peterson's Guides, Inc.
P.O. Box 2123
Princeton, NJ 08543
609/243-9111

Telecommunications

Telecommunications Directory
Gale Research, Inc.
835 Penobscot Building
Detroit, MI 48226
800/877-8638

Transportation

Moody's Transportation Manual
99 Church Street
New York, NY 19997
212/553-0300

Travel

World Travel Directory
Travel Weekly
Reed Travel Group
500 Plaza Drive
Secaucus, NJ 07096
201/902-2000

Congratulations! Having finished this book,
you're well on your way to a lifetime of perfect pitches—
and the job of your dreams.

For more information on David Andrusia's seminars,
newsletters, and personal appearances, or to schedule a one-
on-one career counseling session, please write to:

David Andrusia
PERFECT PITCH LTD.
1318 Havenhurst Drive, #10
West Hollywood, CA 90046
or call:
(213) 656-1464

About the Author

DAVID ANDRUSIA is a career consultant who has helped clients in all fields get the jobs of their dreams. A graduate of Columbia University and the Sorbonne, he earned his master's degree at the Annenberg School of Communications at the University of Pennsylvania, and studied marketing at the Wharton School. Andrusia has held executive posts at Revlon, Swatch Watch USA, and New Line Cinema, where he was head of marketing for the home video group. He lives in Los Angeles and New York.